Anxiety and Phobia

WORKBOOK

Manage Anger, Stress, and Fear. Eliminate Negative Thoughts and Learn to Overcome Anxiety in Work, Life, and Relationship

By William Richards

CONTENTS

INTRODUCTION

The word anxiety , from the Latin angered meaning "to tighten", communicates very well the feeling of discomfort experienced by those who suffer from one of the disorders related to their spectrum, or the idea of constraint, embarrassment and uncertainty about the future. L ' anxiety, in fact, is a state characterized by feelings of fear and not related concern, apparently, to some specific stimulus, unlike the fear that assumes a real danger.

Anxiety: history of the term

The ancient Greeks called it melancholy and thought it derived from an excess of black bile present in the body. This idea, supported by Hippocrates and accepted by Aristotle, was curiously treated with wine, a natural remedy for the physiological symptoms manifested. Only from the Middle Ages onwards was anxiety conceived as a mental and spiritual illness, which religion can remedy through the redemption of the patient's sins. Although medical-biological research will develop during the Enlightenment, many remedies such as decoctions, bloodletting, the use of opium and precious stones, will continue to play a primary role in the treatment of anxiety symptoms among the population. Only from 800 onwards will anxiety be progressively conceived as a mental illness to be treated with drugs and psychotherapy, to be understood etymologically as "therapy of the soul".

Difference between anxiety and fear: distinguish them and understand their value

L ' anxiety is different from fear, because fear is a functional reaction to face an immediate danger while the' Anxiety aims to address a concern about the verifiability of a future event. Psychologists emphasize this aspect of "immediacy" typical of fear, in contrast to the act of "anticipation" that characterizes anxiety. It should be stressed that anxiety and fear are not necessarily "bad" sensations, but on the contrary have an adaptive role. Fear, in fact, is fundamental in the "fight or flight" response, which allows us to mobilize all our resources to face the threat or, alternatively, to flee from it. For this reason, under the right circumstances a fear reaction can save our life. Likewise, anxiety helps us to identify future threats and to guard against them by designing hypothetical scenarios in which we might be involved and, if so, we should face the feared situation. In fact, as the law of Yerkes and Dodson (1908) teaches us, a right degree of anxiety (therefore not excessive) allows us to be more efficient than when we are calm. However, in humans, but also in animals, anxiety often goes beyond its adaptive, useful, aspects to other non-adaptive ones, as anxious reactions are generalized to a series of 'neutral' situations.

Anxiety disorders: when the discomfort becomes clinically relevant

According to the indications provided in the Diagnostic and Statistical Manual of Mental Disorders, anxiety disorders differ from normal developmental fear or anxiety because they are excessive or persistent (typically lasting 6 months or more) with respect to the stage of development.

Many anxiety disorders develop in childhood and tend to persist when left untreated. Most are more commonly found in the female population, with a ratio of 2: 1 to males. It should also be noted that, according to the DSM-5 criteria, any anxiety disorder is diagnosed only when the symptoms are not attributable to the physiological effects of a substance / drug or to another medical condition, or are not better explained by another mental disorder. Here is a short list of anxiety disorders categorized by DSM-5 with their prevalence in the general population (APA, 2013):

Separation Anxiety Disorder (children: 4%; adolescents: 1.6%)
Selective Mutism (between 0.03 - 1%)
Specific phobia (USA: 7 - 9%; Europe: around 6%; Asian, African and Latin American countries: 2 - 4%)
Disorder' social anxiety (phobia social) (USA: 7%; Europe: 2.3%)
Panic Disorder (USA and some European countries: 2.3%; Asian, African and Latin American countries: 0.1 - 0.8%)
Agoraphobia (1.7%)
Generalized anxiety disorder (US: 2.9%, other countries: 0.4 - 3.6%)
Substance / Drug Induced Anxiety Disorder (0.002%)
Anxiety Disorder Due to another Medical Condition (Ns)
Anxiety disorder with other specification (ns)
Unspecified anxiety disorder (ns)

Symptoms of anxiety
L ' anxiety is manifested through physiological forms:

Increased heart rate.
Increased concentration to face the threat.
Attack - escape.

In detail, the anxiety symptomatology , which manifests itself with greater severity in Panic Disorder, includes: palpitations, heart palpitations or tachycardia , increased sweating, fine or large tremors, dyspnoea or a feeling of suffocation, feeling of suffocation, pain or discomfort chest pain, nausea or abdominal distress, feelings of dizziness, of instability, "light-headed" or faintness, chills or hot flushes, paresthesia (numbness or tingling sensations), derealization (feelings of unreality) or depersonalization (being detached from themselves), fear of losing control or "going crazy" and fear of dying.

The symptoms of the anxiety in question, as anticipated, appear among the diagnostic criteria of Panic Disorder in the DSM-5, so they do not necessarily occur in all patients suffering from anxiety and in any case they can decline differently depending on the subject in question. It is fair to speak of a panic attack when the subject experiences sudden intense fear or discomfort that peaks within minutes, accompanied by four or more of the symptoms listed above.

Generalized anxiety disorder

Restlessness (feeling tense, with nerves on the skin), fatigue, difficulty concentrating or memory lapses, irritability, muscle tension and sleep disturbances (difficulty falling or staying asleep, or restless and unsatisfactory sleep).

What makes it possible to draw a border between pathological and non-pathological is the excessive dimension of the worries and the negative impact they have on the psychosocial functioning of the individual. According to the World Health Organization, 5% of the world population, mainly women, suffers from generalized anxiety disorder. However, only a third of those who suffer from it go to a mental health specialist, as the physical symptoms of anxiety often lead patients to turn to other professionals (e.g. general practitioner, internist, cardiologist, pulmonologist, and gastroenterologist).

The social anxiety disorder

The Social Anxiety Disorder (or Social Phobia), however, is characterized by a fear or anxiety marked relative to one or more social situations in which the individual is exposed to possible consideration of others. What the individual really fears is the possibility of acting in such a way as to manifest his anxiety symptoms, which will be evaluated negatively (because embarrassing, humiliating, will lead to rejection or will be offensive to others). As in many anxiety disorders, the anxiety-inducing situations are avoided or endured with discomfort to the patient.

The fear, anxiety and avoidance to diagnose social anxiety must last more than 6 months and must be disproportionate to the real threat posed by the situation.

TYPES

The category of anxiety disorders includes a variety of different disorders. For a long time these disorders were considered, in the wake of Freudian conceptualizations, forms of neurosis. These disorders were conceptualized thanks to the clinical work done by Sigmund Freud on his patients; consequently, the diagnostic category of neuroses came to be closely connected with psychoanalytic theory. Over time, many therapists began to question the validity of the term "neurosis", because it became too broad and all-encompassing, and risked losing its meaning. Starting with the third version of the DSM (Diagnostic and Statistical Manual of Mental Disorders), and especially in the fourth (and last, in the present state), the old categories of neuroses are redistributed among new and more precise diagnostic categories; these include anxiety disorders.

For anxiety today will mean the apprehensive anticipation of future danger or a negative event, accompanied by feelings of dysphoria and physical symptoms of tension.

Anxiety, taken by itself, is a completely normal phenomenon as it is an emotion that prepares and activates the body in situations that could be dangerous.

Instead, it becomes an unpleasant emotional disorder when the state of alarm and fear is "exaggerated" compared to the real dangers or if the dangers are not there at all.

In this case, anxiety is not adaptive, but becomes a problem that can make the person unable to control their emotions and to deal with even the simplest situations. We can therefore distinguish two types of anxiety; those called state and those called tract.

State anxiety is conceptualized "as a transient emotional state or as a condition of the human organism, characterized by subjective feelings perceived at a conscious level of tension and apprehension, and by the increased activity of the autonomic nervous system. It can vary over time and fluctuate over time" (Spielberger et al., 1970).

Trait anxiety, on the other hand, refers to "relatively stable individual differences in the disposition towards anxiety, that is, differences between people in the tendency to respond with elevations in the intensity of state anxiety to situations perceived as threatening" (Spielberger et al., 1970).

Anxiety disorders are characterized by the fact that the most relevant symptom is fear, or anxiety. Although fear and anxiety can have the value of synonyms, we tend to use the term "fear" in reference to a concrete and present stimulus or event, while we tend to use "anxiety" to indicate that the stimulus or event triggering is vague, unidentifiable, or projected into the future.

The anxiety disorder may be a psychological discomfort to self standing unit or be a symptom of other psychological disorders (for e.g. Depression).

It can manifest itself on an emotional level as an apprehensive expectation, accompanied by worry and insecurity, anticipation of negative events; and at a somatic level with increased heart rate, sweating, muscle spasms, paleness, tremors, dizziness, and in the most extreme cases, flight reactions, and immobilization, a feeling of suffocation or chest tightness.

The anxiety disorders, according to DSM-IV, include the following diagnostic categories:

- Panic disorder (with or without agoraphobia);

- Agoraphobia without a history of panic disorder;
- Specific phobia ;
- Social phobia ;
- Disorder obsessive - compulsive disorder;
- Disorder post-traumatic stress disorder;
- Disorder acute stress disorder;
- Generalized anxiety disorder ;
- Disorder anxiety due to a general medical condition;
- Substance induced anxiety disorder ;
- Disorder anxiety not otherwise specified.

Anxiety Classification and Care. The Generalized Anxiety Disorder

Generalized anxiety disorder is characterized by chronic and excessive anxiety and worry. We speak of "generalization", because anxiety and worries concern a large number of events and activities, which are processed as potentially dangerous, rather than a limited number of specific situations.

The "disturbance" is considered such when:

Anxiety and worry cause clinically significant distress or impairment in social, occupational or other important areas;

Anxiety and concerns occur most days for at least six months and the person has difficulty in "control" the concern.

At least three of these symptoms must be present in the disorder:

- Restlessness;
- Easy fatigue;
- Difficulty concentrating or memory lapses;
- Irritability;

- o Muscle tension;
- o Sleep disturbance.

People with generalized anxiety disorder, unlike other anxiety disorders, have great difficulty remembering the onset of their disorder, and very often report that the main symptoms were already present in them in childhood; stressful life events also seem to play some role in its onset (Blazer, Hughes & George, 1987). Generalized anxiety disorder also has a high degree of co-morbidity with other anxiety disorders or mood disorders.

Anxiety Classification and Care. Post Traumatic Stress Disorder

This disorder is a consequence of extreme traumatic events experienced by the person. Events that cause death, threaten death or cause very serious injury or threaten the physical integrity of the person or others, to which the person witnesses with feelings of helplessness, horror and very strong fear, thus causing a high reaction of anxiety.

During and after exposure to stressful events, dissociative symptoms may occur, such as:

- o Subjective feeling of numbness, detachment, or absence of emotional reactivity;
- o Reduced awareness of the surrounding environment and stunning;
- o Derealization;
- o Depersonalization;

- o Dissociativeamnesia, that is, the inability to remember some particular aspect of the trauma.

A characteristic symptom of this disorder is the tendency to relive the traumatic event over and over again. The person experiences dissociative states, or experiences feelings of reliving the experience, illusions, hallucinations, dissociative episodes of flashbacks. Another crucial behavior of the disorder is the avoidance of stimuli associated with the event and the attenuation of general reactivity. The person tries to avoid thinking about the trauma or being exposed to stimuli that could bring it back to mind. The lowering of general reactivity manifests itself in diminished interest in others, in a sense of detachment and estrangement, and in the inability to feel positive emotions. These symptoms seem to be contradictory with those exposed a little above; in reality, post-traumatic stress disorder is characterized by fluctuation, that is, by passing through alternating phases in which the person forgets the traumatic experience and others in which it resurfaces violently. Finally, there are symptoms of increased physiological activation. These symptoms include difficulty falling asleep or staying asleep, difficulty concentrating, hyper vigilance, and exaggerated alarm responses. Laboratory studies have confirmed these clinical symptoms by documenting the increase in physiological reactivity in patients with post-traumatic stress disorder; increase aimed at fighting the images produced by their mind and the remarkable intensity of their alarm responses. This symptom can, in most of the cases resolved favorably in a short time, with one adequate support. In other cases, however, the symptomatology persists and interferes with the normal individual, social and working functioning of the subject. In these cases, where the disorder persists beyond four weeks following the trauma and persists for over a month, it is referred to as post-traumatic stress disorder. Many people find themselves experiencing traumatic experiences, but not all develop PTSD. A recent study, for example, found that only 25% of people who went through a traumatic event resulting in physical injury had subsequently developed the disorder. It can therefore be concluded that the event itself cannot be the sole cause of the disturbance. Currently research in this field are trying to determine what factors distinguish individuals following a severe trauma develop post-traumatic stress disorder from those who do not develop.

Anxiety Classification and Care. Disorder of Panic

The panic disorder is characterized by a ' intense apprehension, fear and terror to relive a panic attack, during which the following symptoms may be warned:

- o   Palpitation and tachycardia;
- o   Sweating;
- o   Tremors;
- o   Wheezing and choking sensation;
- o   Feeling of asphyxiation;
- o   Chest pain;
- o   Nausea or abdominal discomfort;
- o   Feeling of disarray, derealization and depersonalization;
- o   Fear of losing control and going crazy;
- o   Fear of dying;
- o   Chills and hot flashes.

One of the aspects that make panic attack fundamentally different from other anxiety manifestations is the belief, at least at the time of the attack, of the "physical" nature of the symptom. In fact, in anxiety disorders the emotional aspects are in the foreground, and the physical symptoms are left in the background; while in panic attack patients invariably describe the attack in physical terms, with reference to organs, possible diseases and somatic disorders.

Panic attacks can occur frequently, for example, once to week or even more often; generally they last a few minutes, rarely they last for hours; sometimes they are associated with specific situations, such as driving a car. When strongly associated with situational triggers, they are defined as situation-induced (or situation-induced) panic attacks; when there is a relationship between the exposure to the stimulus and the attack, but less strong than in the previous case, we speak of panic attacks sensitive to the situation. Very often there is a strong anticipation anxiety between one panic attack and the next. Finally, attacks can also occur in the presence of apparently benign mental states, such as during relaxation or sleep, or in situations in which they appear to be completely unjustified; in these cases we speak of unexpected (unprovoked) panic attacks.

According to the directives of the DSM IV, this anxiety disorder involves the presence or absence of agoraphobia. Agoraphobia (from the Greek agora , which means "market square") is a set of various fears that mainly concern public and frequented places, from which it could be difficult to get away or where help may not be available in case that the individual is suffering from a panic attack. Simplifying things a lot, agoraphobia could be summed up as the fear of having a panic attack in an open or public place. There are the fear of going to shops to shop, the fear of being in a crowd and the fear of traveling. People with agoraphobia often experience severe discomfort when leaving home, and may even completely avoid doing so. In these cases we speak of panic disorder with agoraphobia.

Anxiety Classification and Care. Specific Phobia and Social Phobia

A specific phobia is represented by a marked, persistent unreasonable or disproportionate fear of precise stimuli or circumscribed and clearly discernible situations. This fear causes the individual to engage in avoidance behavior, which he recognizes to be unreasonable. Among the most common phobias are:

- The fear of heights (acrophobia);
- The fear of spiders (arachnophobia);
- The fear of snakes (ophidiophobia);
- The fear of blood and wounds (blood phobia);
- The fear of enclosed spaces (claustrophobia);
- The fear of public places and open spaces (agoraphobia);
- The fear of being buried alive (taphophobia);
- And fear of dogs (cynophobia).

Specific phobias are unjustified fears, caused by the presence or expectation of a specific object or situation. Many specific fears do not cause problems so crippling that they prompt the person to seek outside help. If, for example, a person with an extreme fear of snakes lives in a metropolitan area, they will most likely have very little direct contact with the object of their fear, so they will be convinced that they do not suffer from any serious problems. The speech would be very different if the person in question lived in an area where there are a large number of snakes. The term phobia typically implies subjective psychological suffering and impairment of social or occupational functioning as a consequence of anxiety.

Social phobia is characterized by a marked and persistent fear of social or "performance" situations. The person is afraid of acting and behaving inappropriately in the presence of unfamiliar people, of feeling embarrassment, shame and humiliation. Consequently, social situations are avoided, in less serious cases they are tolerated with difficulty. People can experience violent manifestations of gastrointestinal redness, sweating, and discomfort. In addition to anxiety during the exhibition, can manifest an anticipatory anxiety, such as worry about days or hours before a social event difficult to avoid; this can lead to a vicious cycle that self-feeds anxiety.

The DSM-IV distinguishes a subtype of social phobia, defined as "generalized". This subtype refers to the fear of most social interactions; people with this type of phobia may have more problems and difficulties and tend to develop depression, alcoholism and other anxiety disorders. The development of the problem usually dates back to adolescence. The more serious and widespread the problem, the greater its chronicity.

Anxiety Classification and Care. Obsessive Compulsive Disorder

The disorder obsessive-compulsive disorder is a disorder of anxiety in which the mind is invaded by persistent and uncontrollable thoughts, or in which the person is pushed irresistibly to repeat continuously certain acts; the result is considerable psychological distress and significant interference with the activities of daily life.

For obsessions we mean thoughts, impulses or mental images, which are recurrent and persistent, which cause marked anxiety or discomfort and which are experienced by the person concerned as intrusive and inappropriate. The person is perfectly aware that these thoughts are the product of his mind, and therefore tries to "neutralize" them with other thoughts or through actions.

The compulsions are behaviors, such as washing hands repeatedly or checking and rechecking that the person feels compelled to take to reduce the distress that accompanies an obsession or to prevent some dreaded event. The person realizes the unreasonableness of the compulsion and tries to resist it, in vain. The most common compulsions are those related to cleanliness and order.

The disorder obsessive-compulsive disorder is characterized by the presence of obsessions and compulsions that cause marked distress, the person engaging in rituals at least an hour to day and that significantly interfere with the person's normal routine, occupational, academic, and social relations.

LET'S SEE THE PHOBIAS IN DETAIL

The phobias are fears of proportion to something that does not represent a real danger, but the person perceives this state of anxiety as uncontrollable, even by implementing behavioral strategies help you cope.

Those who suffer from phobias, in fact, are overwhelmed by the terror of coming into contact with what they fear: a spider or a lizard, etc.

Symptoms of Phobias

The physiological symptoms experienced by those suffering from phobias are: tachycardia, dizziness, gastric and urinary disorders, nausea, diarrhea, suffocation, redness, excessive sweating, tremor and fatigue. Obviously, these pathological manifestations take place only at the sight of the feared thing or at the thought of being able to see it.

Phobias & Avoidance

The phobic , are substantially of anxious and as such work, in the sense that they tend to avoid situations associated with fear, but in the long run this mechanism becomes a real trap. In fact, the avoidance only confirms the danger of the avoided situation and prepares for the following avoidance. Thus a vicious circle is created, which on the one hand leads to being disheartened in one's abilities and on the other compromises social relations, because in order to avoid the feared thing you are ready to give up an evening with friends. For example, those with a phobia of needles and syringes can give up medical checks; those who are afraid of pigeons do not cross the squares, those who fear dogs will avoid all situations in which they will be present, and so on.

Main types of Phobias

There are generalized phobias, such as agoraphobia, fear of open spaces, and social phobia, fear of exposing oneself in public, and specific phobias, generally managed by avoiding the feared stimuli, which can be:

Situational type.

Phobia of spiders (arachnophobia), phobia of birds or phobia of pigeons (ornithophobia), phobia of insects, phobia of dogs (cynophobia), phobia of cats (ailurophobia), phobia of mice, etc ..

Natural environment type.

Phobia of temporal (brontofobia), phobia of heights (acrophobia), of the dark phobia (scotofobia), phobia of water (hydrophobia), etc.

Type blood-injection-injury.

Phobia of the blood (blood phobia), phobia of needles, syringes phobia, etc...

In this case the fear is triggered by other stimuli such as: the fear of situations that could lead to contracting a disease etc. There is a particular form of phobia concerning one's body or parts of it that the person perceives as disproportionate, unwatchable, horrible compared to how they really show themselves (dysmorphophobia).

The phobias do not conceal any symbolic meaning unconscious and fear is simply linked to involuntary incorrect learning experiences against something. In this case, the organism automatically associates the dangerousness with an object or situation that is objectively not dangerous.

This association occurs by classical conditioning, i.e. the relationship between thought and object is created thanks to the first frightening exposure that occurred and is maintained over time due to the avoidance put in place in order not to experience that terrible emotion of strong anxiety that follows. .

SYMPTOMS

Anxiety and anxiety disorders

Anxiety is the emotion felt in front of a feeling of threat or figured that aims to prepare ourselves to face the perceived danger.

Anxiety definition

Anxiety is the emotion felt in front of a sense of threat (The threat to the person) or figurative (The threat to self-esteem).

Physical symptoms of anxiety: due to a neurovegetative hyperactivation , they consist of palpitations, tachycardia, sweating , throat spasms, dyspnoea, dizziness, frequent urge to urinate, gastrointestinal symptoms, insomnia with difficulty falling asleep and frequent awakenings.

Motor tension: tremors, restlessness, agitation, ease of wincing, muscle contractures, tension headache.

It is possible to distinguish several **types of anxiety**:

Automatic anxiety: innate response to an internal or external danger;

Acquired anxiety: it is the type of anxiety without any provocation.

Anticipatory anxiety: it has a short duration and is triggered by a real or imaginary, identifiable signal associated with danger;

Generalized anxiety: it is a feeling of lasting tension not associated with particular stimuli;

Panic attacks: these are intense anxiety attacks that resolve quickly, during which you feel a sudden sense of grave danger (fear of dying, fear of going crazy, and fear of losing control). They are characterized by a very marked somatic activation, with intense physical symptoms such as palpitations, air hunger, and dizziness up to a sense of alienation from reality.

Anxiety Problems

L ' anxiety is an emotion present in a transversal manner in different syndromes and psychiatric disorders; we could say that there is practically no disorder in which anxiety problems do not occur at a stage of its course: anxiety problems are present in disorders related to substance use, which often develop as an attempt to self-medicate towards strong anxiety; disturbing and intense experiences of anxiety characterize psychosis, as well as the deep phases of depression or manic activation ; l ' anxiety develops as a secondary problem in disorders somatoform , in sexual disorders (eg. performance anxiety) and in most of organic diseases; in obsessive compulsive disorder , obsessions (thoughts, images, fears, intrusive and persistent impulses that the individual cannot get rid of from their mind) generate such anxiety in the person as to induce them to perform rigid behavioral or mental rituals (compulsions) with the aim of reducing and / or neutralizing anxiety ; in related stress disorders , such as post-traumatic stress disorder and acute stress disorder, the subject continually relives the memory or image of traumatic events that are particularly relevant to him, all accompanied by strong anxiety and marked neurovegetative activation.

If the disorders mentioned above the problems of anxiety are present despite not being its core, the ' anxiety represents the main feature of two groups of disorders identified in the DSM-5: the anxiety disorders, classified on Axis I, and disorders personality of group C or anxious cluster, classified on Axis II, in which we find themes similar to those of the main Axis I anxiety disorders.

Where to contact Techniques and therapies

In the latest edition of the Diagnostic and Statistical Manual of Mental Disorders, the following disorders are classified as anxiety disorders:

- Separation Anxiety Disorder
- Selective mutism
- Specific Phobia
- Social anxiety disorder
- Panic Disorder
- Agoraphobia
- Generalized anxiety disorder
- Medical condition anxiety disorder
- Other specific anxiety disorder
- Anxiety disorder not otherwise specified

An anxiety disorder can only be diagnosed when it is determined that the anxiety symptoms are not attributable to the physiological effects of a substance or drug or another medical condition, or are not better explained by another mental disorder.

Many anxiety disorders develop in childhood and tend to persist when left untreated. Most are more commonly found in the female population, with a ratio of 2: 1 to males. Below we indicate the prevalence in the general population of major anxiety disorders reported in DSM-5:

Separation Anxiety Disorder (children: 4%; adolescents: 1.6%)
Selective mutism (between 0.03 - 1%)
Specific phobia (USA: 7 - 9%; Europe: around 6%; Asian, African and Latin American countries: 2 - 4%)
Social anxiety disorder (phobia social) (USA: 7%; Europe: 2.3%)
Panic Disorder (USA and some European countries: 2.3%; Asian, African and Latin American countries: 0.1 - 0.8%)
Agoraphobia (1.7%)
Generalized anxiety disorder (US: 2.9%, other countries: 0.4 - 3.6%)
Substance / Drug Induced Anxiety Disorder (0.002%)

Co-morbidity of anxiety disorders

The anxiety disorder can occur in co-morbidity, which is in association with a 'further pathology, usually of different origin, during the clinical course of the latter. The diseases most frequently associated with d 'disorders anxiety are depression above all, bipolar disorders, the' ADHD, respiratory diseases, heart and gastrointestinal, l 'arthritis and hypertension (Sareen et al., 2006). Furthermore, it is well established that patients with other diseases co-morbid with anxiety disorders have a worse course of the disorder and a lower quality of life than patients who present exclusively with an anxiety disorder.

It is absolutely important to recognize the presence of any co-morbidity of anxiety disorders to determine which is the pharmacological treatment most suitable in the light of the various disorders.

From physiological anxiety to anxiety disorders

L ' anxiety is an emotion that all of us have experienced in the face of perceived threat, but that does not necessarily imply that has subsequently developed an anxiety disorder. Normally when we feel anxiety we put in place strategies to reduce or eliminate the threat, thus restoring the previous situation to normal. So what causes physiological anxiety to turn into pathological anxiety and structure an anxiety disorder? In anxiety disorders, the physiological activation that follows the perception of a threat in the environment is in turn assessed catastrophically by the subject, becoming itself a threat, often even more serious than the external threat that has acted as a trigger. Thus a vicious circle is created in which the misinterpretation and catastrophic interpretation of the symptoms of anxiety increases the unpleasant sensations and these in turn reinforce the catastrophic interpretation. The anxiety disorder is thus maintained by:

Selective attention: The subject pays extreme attention to the signals of his own body interpreting them in a catastrophic way;

Brooding: The subject spends a lot of time worrying trying to predict or prevent negative events in conditions of uncertainty and mentally constructing hypothetical solutions without ever reaching a conclusion;

Avoidance: The subject avoids the feared stimuli in order not to incur anxiety, thus reducing their degrees of freedom.

Anxiety attacks and panic attacks: similarities and differences

Sometimes people think that anxiety attacks and attacks of panic are the same thing. However, from a clinical perspective, panic and anxiety have different characteristics and specific symptoms.

For this reason it is good to distinguish them and know how they are experienced by people.

The "Anxiety Attacks"

In summary, "Anxiety attack " is not a clinical term, but it is used by many people to describe a feeling of intense malaise in which they worry about an upcoming event or experience feelings of dread or fear that do not satisfy their needs. Diagnostic criteria for a panic attack.

Anxiety is highly correlated with excessive concern for potential "dangers" or future threats, and symptoms may be similar to those of a panic attack, albeit of lower intensity.

The most common anxiety disorders, mentioned in the Diagnostic and Statistical Manual of Mental Disorders (DSM-5 American Psychiatric Association):

- Generalized anxiety disorder (GAD)
- Panic Attack Disorder (PAD)
- Specific Phobia
- Social Phobia

It is normal to be worried, tense or frightened if we are under pressure or have to deal with a stressful situation. Anxiety is our body's natural response to danger, an automatic alarm that goes off when we feel threatened.

Although it can be unpleasant, anxiety does not always take on a negative connotation. In fact, it can help us stay alert, focused, push us to action and motivate us to solve problems. But when it becomes constant, intrusive, when it interferes with interpersonal activities and relationships, the functional and adaptive limit is exceeded, and anxiety disorders can develop.

- o How do you feel?
- o Are you constantly tense, worried, on edge?
- o Does the anxiety you feel interfere with work, school or family responsibilities?
- o Are you conditioned by fears that you know are irrational, but cannot get rid of them?
- o Do you think something bad is going to happen if some things didn't go as they should?
- o Do you avoid everyday situations or activities because they make you anxious?
- o Do you experience sudden and unexpected feelings of panic?
- o Do you think that dangers and catastrophes are around every corner?

If you recognize yourself in any of these symptoms it is possible that you suffer from an anxiety disorder.

Anxiety Symptoms

The anxiety disorders are made up of a group of disorders rather than a single disease, therefore, may differ from person to person. One person may suffer from intense anxiety attacks that break out without warning, while another begins to feel sick just at the idea of attending a party. Others may struggle with an extreme fear of driving or be overwhelmed by the idea of seeing a spider. Still others may live in a constant state of tension, worrying about everything and everyone.

Despite the different types, all anxiety disorders share a prevalent symptom of severe and persistent fear or worry in situations in which other people would not feel threatened.

Emotional and physical symptoms of anxiety:

Anxiety is more than just a feeling. It is a product of the body's fight-or-flight response and encompasses a wide range of physical symptoms. Due to the many unpleasant sensations, anxiety sufferers often confuse their disorder with a physical illness. It can lead to numerous medical visits and to hospital several times before the anxiety disorder is identified.

In addition to the main symptom of excessive and irrational worry and fear, other common symptoms of anxiety include:

- Emotional symptoms
- Tachycardia
- Sweating
- Upset stomach
- Need to urinate frequently or diarrhea
- Shortness of breath
- Muscle tremors or twitches
- Muscle tension
- Migraines
- Fatigue
- Insomnia
- Physical symptoms
- Feeling of apprehension - threat
- Difficulty concentrating
- Voltage
- Tendency to anticipate negative events
- Irritability
- Agitation
- Tendency to look for signs of danger
- Feeling light-headed
- There are several types of anxiety disorders, each of which with its own symptom profile

How long does an anxiety attack last?

Another important distinction between a panic attack and an anxiety attack is duration. Unlike panic, the symptoms of which are immediate, those of anxiety can be persistent and last for days, weeks or even months.

Helping those suffering from anxiety attacks?
Whether that it is panic attacks, persistent anxiety or both, effective treatment is always to Cognitive Behavioral.
The international guidelines for the treatment of anxiety disorders recommend the Cognitive Behavioral Techniques to learn strategies to manage anxiety or panic moments.

Clinical Differences between Panic Disorder and Anxiety
Psychologists base their diagnoses on the definitions in the Diagnostic and Statistical Manual of Mental Disorders (DSM-5). The latter uses the term "panic attack" for symptoms associated with Panic Disorder. But crises can also occur in association with other psychological disorders.
The term "anxiety attack "is not present in the DSM-5. Rather, anxiety is used to describe a fundamental characteristic of many conditions included in the macro category of "Anxiety Disorders", namely:

- Separation anxiety disorder
- Selective mutism
- Specific phobia
- Social anxiety disorder (phobiasocial)
- Disorder attacks Panic
- Agoraphobia
- Generalized Anxiety Disorder
- Anxiety disorder induced by substances / drugs
- Disorder anxiety due to another medical condition

The same component anxious is so even a major part in the disorder obsessive-compulsive disorder, the disorder post-traumatic stress disorder (PTSD) and Anxiety Disorder (Hypochondria).

Panic attacks and moments of intense anxiety have differences in quantitative and qualitative terms:

The panic attack

The essential feature of a panic attack is the sudden onset of fear or discomfort that peaks within minutes, during which time four and more than 13 physical or cognitive symptoms occur such as: palpitations or tachycardia, excessive sweating, tremors or shaking, wheezing or choking feeling, chest pain or discomfort, nausea or abdominal pain, shortness of breath, difficulty in breathing or disturbing, feeling dizzy or faint, shivering or flushing, numbness or tingling sensations, feelings of unreality (derealization) or detachment from oneself (depersonalization), fear of losing control or going crazy and fear of dying.

Usually the panic attack is distinguished from moments of intense anxiety by the time it takes to reach the peak of intensity which usually occurs within a few minutes and by the greater severity of the symptoms. During a panic attack, the latter are sudden and extremely intense, occur within 10 minutes and then their intensity is lowered. However, some attacks can last longer or occur in succession, making it difficult to determine when one attack ends and another begins. Finally, after an attack, it is not unusual to feel worried or upset for the rest of the day. Some patients describe feelings of exhaustion and a train even several hours later.

CAUSES

The characteristics of Generalized Anxiety Disorder

Characteristic of Generalized Anxiety Disorder is the manifestation of anxiety-inducing symptoms that are protracted over time, even in the absence of real factors or external events that trigger them. These anxiety-inducing symptoms consist of restlessness, feeling "with nerves on the surface", constant fatigue, difficulty concentrating or memory lapses, easy irritability, muscle tension and sleep disturbances (difficulty falling asleep, maintaining or satisfying general sleep).

These signs are normal in certain stressful situations or in particular periods of life, if transient, but they constitute a generalized anxiety disorder when three (or more) of these symptoms occur almost daily, continuously for at least six months.

As a result, the individual has difficulty controlling worry, manifests significant distress and impaired functioning in the social, occupational, family and most important areas of his life.

Diagnosis of Generalized Anxiety Disorder

To diagnose Generalized Anxiety Disorder, anxiety symptoms and constant worries should not be confused with the result of the effects of particular substances, such as drugs or drugs, or the consequence of certain medical conditions (e.g. hyperthyroidism) . A strong state of anxiety is often found even in people who suffer from other psychological disorders, but in this case the symptoms may be the effect or expression of pathology and not the primary cause of the reported malaise.

From a clinical point of view, those who suffer from generalized anxiety experience a constant state of worry about even unimportant events or activities that they fear they cannot manage, or for dangers very far from everyday life and which occur rarely, but which are perceived as imminent and threatening. It is common that due to Generalized Anxiety Disorder a person may, for example, exaggerate an earthquake while living in a non-seismic area, or may give up taking the car for fear of getting lost in a new road and at the same time avoid public transport for fear of not knowing which stop to get off at. These worries are perceived as very difficult to control, so much so that they interfere with normal daily activities, often hindering the person's ability to concentrate and preventing them from completing the tasks they were doing.

The typical thoughts of those suffering from Generalized Anxiety Disorder are related to different areas: the routines to be performed, the responsibilities, the economic issues, their health, that of family members, the misfortunes that can happen. All of this significantly interferes with psychosocial functioning, because the object of concern is constantly shifting from one domain to another. In fact, if a particular concern (such as being late for an appointment) is denied (arriving on time), another one immediately arises that traps the person by engaging him with other thoughts, as if it were impossible to reassure. Regardless of external events, even living in a very quiet reality, Generalized Anxiety Disorder makes every event or situation perceive as a possible threat. Being always in a state of alert is also expensive not only from a mental point of view, but also physical : tremors, contractures and muscle aches are common consequences of this disorder along with somatic symptoms such as excessive sweating, nausea and diarrhea that contribute to creating a general state of tension very harmful to health.

The Generalized Anxiety Disorder, to be diagnosed properly, should not be confused with similar anxiety-inducing situations: it must not be due to other medical conditions or be the result of pharmacological effects. In the latter case, for example, the disorder would disappear once the effect of the substance / drug is over: if, for example, an exaggerated consumption of coffee generates anxiety symptoms, these should be considered as anxiety induced by an excess of caffeine.

Social Anxiety Disorder (or Social Phobia) similarly manifests itself in symptoms, but affects the individual only before a performance or before coming into contact with other people, therefore in social situations where one is exposed to the judgment of others.

Anxious symptoms are also found in Obsessive Compulsive Disorder: in this case, however, they are generated by particular obsessions (inappropriate ideas) that create compulsions (unusual behaviors) in the individual to control and calm anxiety. In this case there is no general concern for future events: anxiety is focused on very specific thoughts and obsessions.

Anxiety symptoms are also well present in post traumatic stress disorder. It occurs when an individual suffers a serious trauma that has put his life at risk (a serious accident, war experiences, etc.) or has witnessed similar events involving other people. The anxiety-inducing symptoms in this case, however, are related to the post-traumatic disorder and are not attributable to a state of generalized anxiety.

The onset of the disorder is therefore quite late even if there are, albeit rarely, forms of generalized anxiety even in adolescence.

Symptoms are pervasive and persistent, usually with a fluctuating trend over the course of life. The content of the worries is often correlated with the age and life reality of the person who suffers from it: adults tend to worry in an exaggerated way for the well-being and health of their family, for economic issues related to everyday life o for the safety of the children; typical of the elderly are concerns related to deficiencies due to age, fear of falling or not being self-sufficient. The Generalized Anxiety Disorder can get to determine protective behaviors, such as limiting leave home, avoid driving, to be alone.

Causes of Generalized Anxiety Disorder

The origin of Generalized Anxiety Disorder is specific to each individual who suffers from it. The literature identifies possible areas of vulnerability that can contribute to the onset of this problem: from a physiological point of view, there is an altered functioning of some brain circuits responsible for regulating the neurotransmitters serotonin and noradrenalin.

Inhibiting certain behaviors or emotions or having a pervasive tendency to avoid the possibility of harm is temperament traits in line with the development of Generalized Anxiety Disorder. From the point of view of the family environment and growth are important proposed educational models, the established relationship and the example provided by the parents. The growing environment plays a fundamental role in preparing the person to effectively manage stress, even if the environmental factor alone is not enough to cause the disturbance. Genetic predisposition is also important, but being genetically predisposed to the disorder does not necessarily mean that it will manifest itself: it is the set of specific factors and conditions that cause the disorder to manifest it.

The expression of Generalized Anxiety Disorder varies greatly depending on the culture of origin: it has been found that it is much easier to develop a generalized anxiety disorder for European individuals at the expense of other non-European cultures. There is also a greater chance of suffering from the disorder living in industrialized countries than in non-industrialized countries.

It therefore seems that the symptomatic manifestation is also linked to habits and context: the assessment of the dangerousness of a situation is guided by the habits of an individual, transmitted to him by the culture to which he belongs and by the daily reality in which he interacts: what is considered stressful for a in fact, an individual may not be so for another.

Psychopathological constructs related to anxiety disorder generalized.

The central element of the disorder is brooding, that is, the constant thinking and rethinking about the negative events that could happen, with the aim of predicting them, preventing them and preparing to face them. The brooding concerns the concern about future events, perceived as dangerous, for which the individual feels the need to prepare, to find possible solutions to manage these threats. People with Generalized Anxiety Disorder perceive brooding as uncontrollable, unable to stop it although they experience an increase in malaise related to this style of thinking. The brooding, however, is seen by the person anxious as a viable weapon against its symptoms: as pervasive ideas and concerns emerge in his mind all the time, mulling the individual has the impression of being able to prepare to face the situation and to feel thus better sure. In reality, however, it is precisely the act of brooding that further increases the anxiety symptoms, creating a real vicious circle that feeds itself.

Then when the individual suffering from generalized anxiety comes to understand the functioning of brooding and tries to get rid of it, he tends to get distracted, not to think or to seek reassurance: however, these strategies are in the long run deficient, as they maintain and nourish the disorder.

Characteristics and components of anxiety

What comes into play when anxiety sets in? The perception of a danger.

This perception has a neurophysiologic component and a component of thought representation.

To explain the concept in simple terms, we can say that the neurophysiologic perception of a danger occurs according to this scheme:

Thought: *I see a lion and I think I am in danger.*

Feeling: *I feel the emotion of fear. Emotions are a synaptic circuit : they are felt because neurons are activated in a certain way in the body. The pupils of the eyes dilate, the hair stands on end, the hair on the arms rises, the blood pressure rises and the heartbeat too: the nervous system prepares for danger.*

Behavior: *I feel fear and flee.*

Anxiety and environment

Our anxious and fearful reaction can be genetically determined, but it is also linked to the representation of thought. If, for me, being in front of a lion is normal because my parents were tamers at the circus, this condition will not pose a danger. On the other hand, if as a child I was excessively subjected to an atmosphere of fear, and I had a very anxious mom or dad, some of my synaptic circuits remain more easily activated in this sense. Hence, I will more easily enter a state of anxiety.

According to research, anxiety can be learned from the environment: it depends on what we learned in our childhood.

"Our reality is always a representation - adds Dr. Raneri -. Although it is an objective datum, it is always constructed through the senses, therefore through our ability to imagine. So, when we perceive stimuli, if we have learned that these stimuli are a source of danger, we associate them automatically to the anxious type response. If my mother is anxious about new things in general, when I have new things to do, I will probably also get anxious. Furthermore, another important aspect to consider is that, usually, when the person who is structurally anxious thinks he cannot face new things, this anxiety of his depends very much on his idea of himself. He does not feel capable, feeling not capable he gets scared and therefore feels anxiety. "

The causes: hereditary, biological and unconscious factors

The causes of anxiety are diverse and complex. Wanting to make a summary, we can divide the factors that determine more or less severe anxiety states into 3 macro categories:

Hereditary factors: There are genetic studies that have found that, frequently, individuals with anxiety disorders have a family member affected by the same disease.

The biological factors: According to research carried out on the human brain, anxiety could be caused by alterations in the quantity of some neurotransmitters. Thus, the biological site of anxiety seems to be the Locus Coeuruleus, which is responsible for activating or deactivating the inhibitory neurons that are activated by Gamma-Amino butyric Acid (GABA).

The unconscious factors: According to Freud's theory, anxiety is caused by an unconscious conflict.

Freud's unconscious factors:

For Freud - explains Dr. Raneri - anxiety is therefore linked to an intrapsychic aspect, and has two meanings:

It is the manifestation of a neurotic conflict, that is, a struggle between a desire (sexual or aggressive) and the prohibition of the super-ego, aimed at inhibiting the awareness of desire, because it is considered reprehensible.

It is the way to remove awareness of the conflict itself.

So we, failing to get in touch with these unacceptable desires, experience anxiety, as a danger signal of the emergence of those contents that we want to remove. The person feels anxiety, but does not know why: to remove it, he should decode his experience and understand what is frightening him.

Other causes of anxiety

There can then be existential anxieties, which give rise to anxiety, for example with respect to evolutionary phases, such as: I am retiring and I feel anxiety about the future.

"As Fromm said - adds Dr. Raneri - anxiety expresses the distance of contemporary man from himself, or from the fundamental values and needs of the human being, such as having meaningful emotional relationships and expressing oneself in one's social context."

In fact, anxiety derived from a lack of internal security is very common.

"When people have not been able to build the experience of the safe base in their minds, - explains Dr. Raneri - by introjecting into their mind the experience of an adult, usually a parent, who takes care of them and knows how to tune in. with their emotional needs , they often manifest anxiety disorders. In fact, the child, when he experiences a ' caregiver ' who offers safety, gradually memorizes this supportive, comforting and generally positive relationship within himself , bringing it back into his life as an adult. Instead, when this full feeling of security is lacking, anxiety is one of the basic signals related to this situation of generalized insecurity. "

So, to summarize, intrapsychic factors anxiety can be related to:

Internalimpulses, according to Freud's theory;
Existentialanxieties;
Lack of an internalized secure basis.

GENERALIZED ANXIETY DISORDER IN ADULTS

Some think that worrying helps solve problems, others believe it is a good way to be prepared for what can go wrong; still others believe it is inevitable to do so. Each of us has concerns and opinions on how best to address them.

In psychology, the condition of those who are excessively and frequently anxious about a large number of different situations is well known, and is called *Generalized Anxiety Disorder (GAD)*.

The most frequent worries that assail patients who suffer from it are running out of money, losing their job or health, being left by their partner, losing children due to illness or an accident. All fears that concern what is most important to us human beings.

Recognizing Generalized Anxiety Disorder may not be easy because this problem, characterized by intense anxiety and numerous other symptoms, shares some characteristics with other disorders and especially with Obsessive Compulsive Disorder.

Contrary to what one might think, Generalized Anxiety Disorder is quite prevalent throughout the West. According to estimates by the American Psychiatric Association, about 3% of Americans and just fewer than 4% of Europeans suffer from it. According to these data, more than 2 million Italians suffer from this disorder. Women, more than men, receive the diagnosis of GAD: 55% -60% of the total are female.

The brooding in Generalized Anxiety Disorder

People with AGD report that they worry about a large number of eventualities, some relating to the present, others centered on the future. As a result, anxiety stabilizes within excessive values, for many hours a day almost every day.

In the DAG, thoughts that are being mulled over have these characteristics:

They are like links in a chain: they follow one another and, in the worst moments, they can overlap.

They lose clarity and, therefore, the ability to resize them. In this way they feed themselves, becoming difficult to control.

They are invasive: they take away space from other thoughts and occupy the entire horizon of the individual who, very often, ends up not thinking about anything else.

On average, symptoms of Generalized Anxiety Disorder become full-fledged around age 30, although this shouldn't suggest a sudden onset. This, in fact, is only the age at which most people receive the diagnosis, perhaps precisely because it is the time when the disorder manifests itself with more intense and disabling symptoms.

In fact, many of these patients report suffering from anxiety all their life even though as children, perhaps, they did not fully meet the diagnostic criteria of the disorder or their symptoms were underestimated. It should be noted, however, that the lower the age at which the disorder begins, the greater the risk that it gets worse and that the individual develops other psychological disorders in addition.

If left untreated, Generalized Anxiety Disorder tends to become chronic, with symptoms that worsen or regress depending on the period or external stressors.

Separation anxiety in adults is a problem as serious as often underestimated.

This psychological condition occurs when there is a fear of the removal, momentary or definitive, of a person, a pet or even a place or an object. In any case, separation anxiety disorder in adults manifests itself openly with symptoms that include nausea, headache or sore throat.

In the first years of life, this disorder is very common in humans because a child does not yet possess cognitive resources capable of mitigating the effect of stressful situations. Like a divorce, a move, or the death of a family member or pet.

However, even in the case of adults, the main problem with this state of anxiety stems from uncertainty. That is the impossibility of knowing, if and when, the much desired reunification can take place. An often unpleasant and very painful condition, as in the case of the departure of a friend, boyfriend or parent for war, for example.

SYMPTOMS OF SEPARATION ANXIETY IN ADULTS

The main feature of separation anxiety disorder in adults is the excessive worry of being alone. But how do you know in what moment the worry, the fear of loneliness becomes a real anxiety disorder?

According to the *American Psychiatric Association*, separation anxiety occurs when a person has one or more of the following symptoms:

Unusual stress from missing a person or pet.

Fear of being alone.

Continuous need, very intense or frequent, to know where another person is.

In adults, these episodes can last 6 months or more. These are symptoms that can cause significant distress and compromise social interaction, as well as academic or work performance.

Causes of separation anxiety disorder in adults

This psychological condition is triggered by the sudden, and apparently inexplicable, separation of loved ones and close ones. A specific type of anxiety that can be related to other mental disorders, such as delusions (psychotic disorders) or fear of change (autism spectrum disorder).

It is often possible to recognize an adult with separation anxiety disorder because they begin to become overprotective. However, he often expresses his fears about separation or estrangement in an "adult" way.

As mentioned, separation anxiety can originate in childhood, particularly when the first emotional bonds are formed. It can also result from later experiences where unexpected or sudden losses occur. Likewise, people who have been abused or have been victims of parental neglect are also more likely to suffer from it.

Risk factors

Separation anxiety in adults often develops after the loss of a loved one or after a significant event, such as a move to another city, a painful bereavement, or even the start of a college or work experience away from home. The aforementioned divorce can certainly favor the onset of the disorder.

In addition, the likelihood of developing a separation anxiety disorder in adults is greater if it is diagnosed in childhood one. Even people with grown too authoritarian parents may be at higher risk, like those who suffer from disorder obsessive-compulsive disorder.

Separation anxiety disorder is often diagnosed in people who have also been diagnosed with one of the following conditions:

- Generalized anxiety disorder.
- Panic.
- Disorder Post-traumatic stress.
- Social anxiety.
- Personality disorder.

Treatment and cures of separation anxiety disorder
Treatment for separation anxiety disorder in adults is similar to that for treating other anxiety disorders. Possible treatments include:

- Group therapy.
- Cognitive Behavioral Therapies.
- Family therapy.
- Dialectical Behavioral Therapies.
- Medicines, such as antidepressants, anxiolytics or psychotropics.

In any case, both diagnosis and treatment must be determined by a qualified professional. Therefore, whenever you suspect the possible presence of this disorder, you will need to contact a good psychologist.

GENERALIZED ANXIETY DISORDER IN CHILDREN

In developmental age, generalized anxiety disorder (GAD) manifests itself with excessive and uncontrollable worries about a large number of daily events or activities.

Although younger children may show signs of excessive anxiety, generalized anxiety disorder develops at about the age of 12 years.

Although there may be awareness of the excessiveness of their concerns with respect to different situations, children and young people feel they are unable to have control over them.

Generalized anxiety disorder can often appear alongside other disorders including social anxiety, separation anxiety, depression, and attention deficit hyperactivity disorder.

Unlike normal worries, or fears experienced in childhood, the disorder persists for at least six months and causes impaired functioning in the social, school and family settings.

Generalized Anxiety Disorder In Children And Adolescents: How Does It Manifest?

The most frequent concerns in children and adolescents relate to present and future school performance, sports performance, social relationships, physical assaults and natural disasters.

Often young people set high standards in achieving their results and are overly critical of them if they are not achieved. Sometimes children with generalized anxiety disorder are not even willing to try new activities if they do not have the certainty of being up to it or are still inclined to abandon them in the course of work if they feel that their performance is not adequate.

Children with this disorder are often described as "little adults", given their propensity to distress over issues not appropriate for their age (for example, family budget, and the state of health of their grandmother or little brother).

Their worries are often associated with a tendency to perfectionism and strict adherence to rules, which leads them to repeat activities in order to make sure they are perfect (such as rewriting homework for making one small mistake).

To try to alleviate their anxieties, they are prompted to constantly seek reassurance (such as asking a parent to review homework several times to make sure it is perfect) or take controlling attitudes over others (for example by calling parents several times today, to ensure they are well). They worry excessively about their abilities or performance and are therefore constantly seeking approval.

Children and young people with generalized anxiety disorder also have great difficulties in making decisions, tend to social isolation and adopt an attitude of procrastination, that is, they tend to postpone constantly.

A growing number of studies suggest the existence, even in children, of a cognitive vulnerability to generalized anxiety disorder: the intolerance of uncertainty. This means that children and young people vulnerable to anxiety cannot tolerate uncertainty and the inability to control all the possible consequences of future events, and therefore try to predict every possible scenario by asking a multitude of questions to the adult. They are constantly looking for details because they need to know what could happen to them in a given situation.

What is meant by concerns?

Worries are nothing more than thoughts regarding the possible occurrence of negative future events. They usually manifest themselves in the form of questions starting with the formula "What if .... "

What if the Italian test goes wrong? I may never be able to learn these things. All my friends will make fun of me. I may not want to go to school anymore. If I don't go to school anymore, I will fail. I'll have to repeat the year. I will no longer have my classmates, I should find new friends. What if they don't accept me in the new class? I will be a failure!

What if I miss an exercise? The professor might tell me I did a bad job. What if he says it in front of the class? Others will laugh at me.

Most children and adolescents with generalized anxiety disorder worry about the same things.

Some of the most common thoughts are:

Health Concerns

"What if I get cold and get sick?"

"What if my mother gets cancer?"

Concerns about school

"What if the math test went wrong?"

"What if I forget what I have to say during my questioning?"

"What if I fail?"

Personal injury concerns

"What if a thief enters the house and harms everyone?"

"And if I came abducted after school?"

Concerns about disasters

"What if there was an earthquake and the house was destroyed?"

"What if there was a flood and I was forced to leave my home?"

Concerns about minor issues

"And if I came teased about my shoes?"

"What if I arrive late for school?"

Generalized Anxiety Disorder At Home: How Does It Manifest?

Below is a list of the most common cognitive, behavioral and physical symptoms experienced by children with Generalized Anxiety Disorder at home:

Concerns regarding school, sports, social, health and family finances performance

- o   Concerns about punctuality

- o Concerns regarding the possible occurrence of earthquakes, wars or other catastrophic events
- o Perfectionism and fear of making mistakes
- o Spending too much time doing homework
- o Lack of self-confidence
- o Continuous requests for approval
- o Requests for reassurance
- o Presence of physical symptoms such as headache, stomach pain, fatigue and muscle aches
- o Sleep disorders
- o Reported feeling of restlessness
- o Irritability
- o Difficulty concentrating
- o Memory lapses
- o Frequent self-criticism
- o Tendency to avoid new experiences
- o Fear of criticism and negative judgments about their abilities.

Tendency to worry excessively about negative events experienced by others for fear that they may happen to them or to their family.

Generalized Anxiety Disorder At School: How Does It Manifest?

At school, a child with generalized anxiety disorder may experience a combination of symptoms listed below.

- o Excessive worry and anxiety about testing
- o Repeated search for the teacher's approval
- o Difficulty speaking in front of the class
- o Difficulty in expressing one's opinion

- o Difficulty getting into class in the morning
- o Delays in entering the school
- o Low self-esteem
- o Difficulty concentrating due to persistent worries
- o Irritability
- o Tendency to avoid difficulties
- o Difficulty completing assigned tasks
- o Frequent memory lapses
- o Refusal to play some games considered dangerous with peers
- o Reluctance to try something new

The Seven Tips for the Family to Manage The Generalized Anxiety Disorder Of Their Son.

Here are some general tips to help your child cope with his generalized anxiety disorder:

Explain to the child what anxiety is. Naming everything they experience calms them down. We tell our child that anxiety is a normal mechanism used by our body to signal danger to us. It is not dangerous and although it is something excessively "annoying", it has a limited duration in time. This system is so efficient that it activates even when there is no real danger, so it ends up giving us a false alarm. It doesn't have to be something to trigger it, just a thought! When our mind continues to produce thoughts, making us believe constantly that we are in danger, the alarm system is activated in many situations until it becomes a problem.

Listen and try to understand his feelings. Try to empathize with your child. Try to understand what emotions and behaviors you would engage in if you constantly lived in fear that something terrible could happen at any moment.

Keep calm. Children perceive their parents' emotions and use them to assess the danger of situations. Staying calm will help them do the same.

Encourage the child not to ask for reassurance. A good way to combat anxiety is to have the child become more comfortable with uncertainty. After all, you cannot assure your child that what he fears will not happen, that his peers will not make fun of him about something or that the verification will be fine. We can't know either! However, we can communicate our confidence that he will be able to face and manage the situation successfully. Not being able to rely on your reassurance, children and young people will have the opportunity to learn new strategies for managing anxiety. This will increase their sense of independence and competence.

Help the child or adolescent find a way to examine the content of their thoughts and to decide on the objective danger of the feared situation. Teach them to consider alternative explanations and scenarios.

Encourage the child's participation in the activities. Avoiding feared situations can be very effective in reducing anxiety in the short term, but in the long term it prevents us from experiencing our ability to cope with it. Your child may want to avoid fun activities, such as attending a birthday party or playing on a sports team. Encourage him to face his fears, participate in games, sports, and make new friends. This will allow him to increase his sense of competence.

Reward your efforts. Reward small achievements. For example, use the occasions when he gives a task to the teacher, asking you only once to check it, to praise and reward him.

THE SCHOOL MANAGEMENT OF THE PUPIL WITH GENERALIZED ANXIETY DISORDER.

There are several ways that school and teachers can help a child or teenager with generalized anxiety disorder. Flexibility and an adequate supportive environment are essential to enable the student with DAG to achieve academic success.

Here are some useful tips for teachers:

Establish good collaboration and communication with the family. It is essential to share the goals and strategies used in managing the child with the family. This will allow you to work in one direction and towards one goal.

- *Accept concerns.* Not devaluing the fears and anxieties of children and adolescents will help them feel understood and not judge themselves negatively.
- *Express trust.* It is important to have confidence in the ability of young people to manage and face their fears. This will help them develop a greater sense of mastery and a positive self-image.
- *Reduce requests.* It may be necessary to reduce the demands placed on children, by scaling down the load of homework, the set of queries and the settings of the tests. For example, it would be useful to prefer multiple choice questions rather than open ones and to prepare scheduled questions, providing clear indications on the part of the program to be studied in depth.

- *Facilitate participation.* Fear of giving the wrong answer or saying something embarrassing or simply feeling the center of attention leads young people not to participate in class activities and discussions. To help them we try to ask them closed questions, in which they have to choose between two alternatives or even give them the opportunity to talk about topics on which they feel confident.
- *Encourage interaction within the class.* Anxious children and teens are easily embarrassed in social situations and tend to remain aloof so as not to attract the attention of others. We try to avoid that the disturbance leads them to distance themselves from friends and push them to isolation; we plan activities to be carried out in small groups.
- *Emphasize successes rather than failures.*
- *Avoid criticism or sarcastic jokes related to performance.*
- *Reward efforts.* Reinforce any efforts made by the child or adolescent who come close to the goals previously agreed upon with the family and professionals involved in the treatment.

The Treatment of Generalized Anxiety Disorder

The treatment of choice for generalized anxiety disorder is cognitive-behavioral therapy.

During the therapy, the support and active collaboration of the parents are fundamental elements, able to influence the results obtained. Their degree of involvement varies according to the age of the child or young people.

Therapy with children makes use of various tools that once learned and used regularly, help overcome generalized anxiety disorder and prevent it from recurring in the future. The most common are:

The identification and modification of dysfunctional thoughts:

Children or teens are taught to identify dysfunctional thoughts related to feared events. Later he will be taught to evaluate situations with greater objectivity, in order to be able to face them with more functional and realistic thoughts.

- *The exhibition.* This technique consists of gradually trying to deal with feared situations. Exposure to feared situations will allow the child or adolescent to verify that these do not involve real danger, also learning that dealing with and managing anxiety is possible.
- *The reinforcement.* Any behavior that the child has, at home, at school or in therapy, and which approaches the set goal, will be rewarded in order to make it more likely to reappear.
- *The modeling.* It is based on the use of the adult as a functional model of behavior in dealing with feared situations.
- *Relaxation and mindfulness techniques.* According to the preferences and characteristics of individual children or adolescents, different relaxation techniques can be used including progressive muscle relaxation, diaphragmatic breathing, autogenic training and relaxation in images. The scientific literature also supports the effectiveness of the use of mindfulness in anxiety disorders in developmental age.
- *Building resilience.* It is taught to children and young people that although they cannot control events, you can

change the impact that they have on them. The use of the techniques learned during the therapy will allow him to face the moments of difficulty, overcome them and to draw useful lessons for the future.

- *The parent training.* Parent involvement in child therapy is of paramount importance. The therapist will teach them how to respond to the requests and behaviors of children or teens, so as not to reinforce their fears and consequently the disorder.

Let's highlight this concept:

SOCIAL ANXIETY DISORDER

Typical symptoms of Social Anxiety Disorder for both children and adults are as follows:

Symptoms of Selective Mutism:

It is a constant inability to speak in specific social situations in which you are expected to speak (e.g. at school) despite being able to speak in other situations. This condition, in the child, interferes with academic achievement or social communication. The duration of the condition is at least 1 month (not limited to the first month of school). The inability to speak is not due to the fact that you do not know, or are not comfortable with, the type of language required by the social situation. The condition is not best explained by the presence of a communication disorder (eg, fluency disorder with onset in childhood) and does not occur exclusively during the course of other disorders (eg, on the autism-spectrum).

Symptoms of separation anxiety disorder

Separation anxiety is a phenomenon normally present during the neuropsychological development of the child who, in general, tends to subside spontaneously after 2 years of age; it typically disappears completely before pubertal development. After six years of age, the persistence of intense separation anxiety from significant figures is worthy of an in-depth study by the psychologist and/or physician specializing in child neuropsychiatry.

The symptoms of separation anxiety are as follows:

- Persistent difficulty leaving parents / caregiver or home.
- Constant and excessive fear that something tragic could happen to a parent / contact person.
- Constant and excessive fear that one may be the victim of an accident or kidnapping while alone.
- Systematic refusal to leave home or to stay home alone.
- Repeated nightmares of separation from parents / contact person or of getting lost in an unknown place.
- Appearance of real or suspected physical symptoms and discomfort, every time you have to leave home or your parents / reference person. For example, the child may complain or suffer from headaches, abdominal pains etc.
- Tendency to be to require constant attention and presence from the parent or a significant figure up to be "sticky" and intrusive.
- Anxious and depressed mood, apathy and disinterest, restlessness and strong melancholy if forced to be alone away from home.

The symptoms must be pervasive and prevent the child suffering from it to devote to common age typical activities (school commitments, Sportici, friendships).

Symptoms must be present for at least 4 weeks in children and adolescents up to 18 years.

Treatment of anxiety disorders in developmental age

The early recognition of an anxiety problem and a correct assumption of the problem may reduce the risk of developing more serious problems at a later stage, or that s pathology.

Already in 1994 Kendall carried out the first randomized and controlled trial to evaluate the efficacy of CBT with anxious children through her "Copingcat" therapy program (16 sessions for children aged 9 to 13). At the end of the program, 64% significant improvements in measures of anxiety symptoms and coping strategies reported by parents. There have been several studies that have followed since then and that have brought evidence of the efficacy of CBT in the treatment of anxiety disorders in children and adolescents. In our studio we apply the Cool Kids Program protocol. It is treatment evidence based and its effectiveness is based on research carried out in a decade at Macquarie University, the Royal North hospital and the Queensland University, the group R.Rapee.

The principles on which the treatment of anxiety disorders is based

The basic principles of cognitive therapy for anxiety disorders with children and adolescents are as follows:

Introduce parents and the child to the concept of the link between situations - thoughts - emotions;

Teach to monitor and identify anxious thoughts;

Explain the effect of cognitive distortions typical of anxious thinking;

Teaching techniques for finding evidence against one's predictions, based on past experience and general knowledge.

Teach to identify and question the consequences of the feared event;

Teaching the ability to generate "calming thoughts" based on a realistic assessment of the anxiety-provoking event.

Learn relaxation techniques.

Gradual exposure and reduction of avoidance behaviors.

ANXIETY AND DEPRESSION

What is depression?

The depression has been called "the evil of the century", he hears about more and more often but not everyone knows really what it is. The depression is a mood disorder, that is, the psychic function that accompanies adaptation to our inner world, the psychological and the external one: the tone is high when we are in pleasant conditions, goes down when we live in unpleasant situations.

The depression is a mood disorder that affects over 350 million people in the world without distinction of sex, age, social status.

Those suffering from depression experience persistent anguish, loss of interest in activities that normally give pleasure and difficulty in carrying out even the simplest daily actions, for at least two weeks, sometimes with negative consequences on interpersonal relationships. However, depression can be prevented and treated - adequate knowledge of depressive disorder can help reduce associated stigma and motivate people to seek help.

People with depression perceive themselves as inadequate and worthless, they view their surroundings as "hostile" and unsupportive, and the future appears uncertain and full of difficulties. Specifically, they experience some of the following symptoms: loss of energy, change in appetite, insomnia or hypersomnia , anxiety, impaired concentration, indecisiveness, restlessness, feelings of worthlessness, guilt or hopelessness, thoughts of self-harm or suicide.

The ideas of death are intrinsic to depressive pathology , characterized by themes of guilt, unworthiness, ruin, and are supported by the belief that there is no other way out of the condition of suffering and that, therefore, the only way to relieve pain. Emotional and no longer represent a burden for others is to commit suicide.

Depression genetic, biological and psychosocial factors

Thinking that depression is due to a single cause is not really correct; it is a multifactorial disorder where genetic, biological and psychosocial aspects interact with each other.

Genetic factors of depression

There are a number of empirical evidences that prove the important hereditary component in depression. Studies show an increased risk (5% - 25%) of developing a similar disorder in first degree relatives of patients with major depression. This does not mean that depression is inevitable, but that you can be vulnerable to the disorder. The genetic factor does not fully explain the occurrence of the disorder.

Biological factors of depression

Depression derives from an alteration in the function of monoaminergic systems (norepinephrine (NA), serotonin (5HT) dopamine), which contribute to the appearance of somatic, cognitive, emotional and relational disorders; both serotonin and norepinephrine carry out their action within brain nuclei responsible for the control of a whole series of functions that are altered in depression (mood modulation, affect regulation, control of some cognitive functions, regulation of sleep and appetite, motivation)

Psychosocial factors of depression

The stressful events favoring the development of depression are experienced by the subject as irreversible, irreparable and total losses. Some of these can be:

- Physical illnesses
- Marital separations
- Difficulty in family relationships
- Serious conflicts and / or misunderstandings with other people
- Important changes of role, home, work,
- Layoffs
- Business or economic failures
- Being the victim of a crime or abuse even as a child
- Loss of a loved one
- Breakup of marriage or engagement
- Problems with justice
- Failures at school

Depressed people feel unable to cope with situations and consider themselves inferior to others and this involves invalidation of the individual and of his entire existential perspective: past, present and future.

The depression left untreated can prevent people to work and to participate in family and social life, to arrive at a real social disability and employment and therefore a heavy impact on the quality of life of the person and those around him next. The American Heart Association (2014) found that depression is associated with an increased risk of developing cardiovascular and cerebrovascular disease. Depression, if left untreated, worsens heart failure outcomes and is associated with higher mortality.

Symptoms Of Depression - What Are The Symptoms Of Depression?

It is correct to speak of depression only when the mood loses its natural character of flexibility, that is, when it is always low and is no longer influenced by favorable external factors, causing discomfort and interfering with normal activities, life and freedom of act of a person.

Characteristic of depression is the tendency to evaluate every situation in a negative and pessimistic way, which is why it represents a pathology of cognitive patterns, thoughts and sensations that make us feel " down in the dumps "; it occurs when you feel that all positive feelings about the future are gone and you feel unable to appreciate the pleasurable aspects of life. The loss of the ability to feel pleasure, joy, affection and amazement takes the name of ANEDONIA: this factor represents the main character of depression.

It is often believed that depression is a simple lowering of mood, instead it must be borne in mind that to characterize depression is a set of symptoms that compromise the way a person thinks, thinks and portrays himself, others and the outside world .

Feeling depressed means seeing the world as if you were wearing glasses with dark lenses: everything becomes gray, dull and difficult to deal with, even carrying out normal daily activities such as getting out of bed, washing, calling a friend, shopping.

The depression , which in the video is called the "black dog" presents different symptoms, such as, lack of appetite, sleeplessness, lack of concentration, irritability, sadness, social isolation, etc., which are to have a heavy impact on quality of life person who suffers from it, to the point of believing that dying is the only way out. Obviously this is not the case: seeking help is essential because healing from depression is possible.

More specifically, depression manifests itself through numerous symptoms, which can be summarized in four broad areas: somatic symptoms, emotional symptoms, behavioral symptoms, cognitive symptoms:

The most common somatic symptoms of depression are:

- o   Loss of energy,
- o   Sense of fatigue,
- o   Impaired concentration and memory,
- o   Motor agitation and nervousness,
- o   Weight loss or gain,
- o   Sleep disturbances (insomnia or hypersomnia),
- o   Lack of sexual desire,
- o   Physical pain,
- o   Sense of nausea.
- o   Typical emotional symptoms of depression in depressed people are:
- o   Sadness,
- o   Anguish,
- o   Despair,
- o   Sense of guilt,
- o   Empty,
- o   Lack of hope in the future,
- o   Loss of interest in any business,
- o   Irritability and anxiety.

The main *behavioral symptoms of depression*, on the other hand, are:

- o   Reduction of daily activities,
- o   Avoidance of people and social isolation,
- o   Passivebehaviors,
- o   Reduction of sexual activity
- o   Suicideattempts.
- o   The main cognitive symptoms, on the other hand, are:
- o   Conceptualslowdown,
- o   Inability to make decisions,
- o   Impaired concentration and memory,
- o   Depressiverumination,
- o   Negative thoughts about yourself, the world and the future,
- o   Ideas of guilt, unworthiness, ruin,
- o   Self-depreciation,
- o   Self-pity,
- o   Perception of slowed down time,
- o   Perception of the current state of mind as an endless condition.

The above is widely supported by DSM 5 (2013), thanks to which it is possible to detail the depressive symptomatology with respect to its course (for example, seasonal) and its severity (mild, moderate, severe). In addition, the DSM 5 can specify the current clinical status of the major depressive disorder or the characteristics of the most recent episode, in complete remission: with mixed manifestations, catatonic, melancholic, atypical, with anxiety, from mild to severe, with serious risk. Suicide and with onset in the postpartum.

Causes of Depression - What Are the Causes of Depression?

The depression is a disease that results from the combination of factors that interact with each other and that varies from person to person. These factors can be grouped into three main categories: genetic, biological and psychosocial factors. It occurs mainly in women and has a strong hereditary component.

Factors which, in combination, can cause depression:

Genetic factors that can cause depression

The genetic hypothesis has been supported by many and numerous studies prove that first degree relatives of patients with major depression have a greater risk of developing the same disorder; obviously it is important to keep in mind that being vulnerable to a disorder does not necessarily mean developing it.

Biological factors that can cause depression

Most of the communication between cells in the nervous system is the work of chemicals called neurotransmitters. Depression would be due to the insufficient activity of some neurotransmitter systems (for example, the monoaminergic ones) and the consequent different functionality of specific brain areas that regulate sleep, appetite, sexual desire and mood. The depression can be connected to a hypersensitivity of the Central Nervous System to changes of estrogen and progestin; both related to the menstrual cycle that childbirth.

Psychosocial factors that can cause depression

The stressful events favoring the development of depression are experienced by the subject as irreversible, irreparable and total losses.

The content of thoughts associated with depression, as Beck himself had already observed, is typically characterized by a negative view of the individual himself, his future and the world. The main themes are failure, inability and hopelessness. In a note, dated January 11, 1965, Beck underlined the presence of three depressogenic cognitive patterns whose main themes were: loss, hopeless and self-blame. Beck will later call these issues "negative expectations about oneself, the world, and the future," concepts that will become known as the "cognitive triad" of depression. The depression can be caused by a single event or a series of events stressors that can cause a sense of discomfort, such as:

- o Physical illnesses
- o Marital separations
- o Difficulty in family relationships
- o Serious conflicts and / or misunderstandings with other people
- o Important changes of role, home, work,
- o Layoffs
- o Business or economic failures
- o Being the victim of a crime or abuse even as a child
- o Loss of a loved one
- o Breakup of marriage or engagement
- o Problems with justice
- o Failures at school

The presence of childhood traumatic experiences can also generate emotional suffering that will lead to a depressed mood, with despair and a sense of helplessness.

Mechanisms for maintaining depression - what are the mechanisms for maintaining depression?

Mechanisms for maintaining depression, what keeps depression?

Depression maintenance factors are those mechanisms that can stabilize and chronicize what could sometimes be an isolated depressive episode.

People who have been depressed react to sadness or a change in mood differently than people who have never been and this depends on a distinctive feature of our memory system. The contexts, in fact, trigger memories: for example, if we are to listen to a song, it can bring out a possible thing of the past that maybe we did not think for years, a place, a person, a special occasion.

Furthermore, it is known that when we learn something new the chances of recalling it are greater if we recall it in the same environment in which we learned it. Applying this same principle to the context of our thoughts and mood, when we feel sad, discouraged or depressed, we will probably also have negative thoughts of self-criticism related to that particular state of mind. So every time we experience a negative emotion again for any reason, our mind will tend to recall those negative thoughts.

In light of this, each time we have another period of depression, the connection between depressed mood and negative thoughts will consolidate, thus raising the probability that the cycle will repeat itself (Siegel, 2012).

Here are the main mechanisms that keep the disorder:

The depressogenic patterns:

The concept of schema highlights why a depressed patient continues to suffer and feel defeated despite the facts show the presence of positive aspects and events in his life. The patterns explain the maintenance of lasting negative attitudes towards oneself, the world, and the future that individuals may have built since childhood. The depressed person will tend to interpret current events as a confirmation of pre-existing depressogenic patterns, selecting and distorting all other available information.

Rumination:

The constant work that the patient does on his depressive thoughts, will lead him to increase and maintain depression because it will make him stay focused on the negative thoughts, responsible for lowering the mood. This process is called rumination: it is a repetitive form of attention paid to oneself, to the fact that one is depressed, to one's symptoms and their causes, meanings and consequences, characterized by recurrence and persistence (Nolen-Hoeksema, 1999); it represents a wrong way, based on emotions and centered on the person, to face the problematic situation that one lives, that is to fight the depressed mood.

Ruminating on thoughts, on losses, on failures, on the way of being, continuously retracing the same thoughts gives only the illusion that sooner or later you will feel better, instead the only thing that rumination leads to is to keep the person focused only on the negative and catastrophic aspects of them, increasing the suffering and therefore the depressed mood .

Evaluation of one's depressive symptoms:

Often, the person suffering from depression tends to criticize and devalue himself precisely because of being depressed, ill, and defective. Sometimes, to avoid this form of personal criticism, the individual tries to implement attempts at solution and takes measures, which however prove useless and can further aggravate the problem itself.

For example, if the depressed person feels tired and without energy, he will reduce his daily activity, without knowing that passivity and inactivity have , instead, the effect of increasing the sense of fatigue, so he will feel even more without energy. And he will be more convinced that he cannot do anything; as a result, her sense of inadequacy will increase, her belief that she is ill, with no way out. This leads the person to isolate himself, keeping at a distance even the closest family members, who could react, in turn, with rejection and criticism; this external response will be interpreted as a confirmation of one's negative beliefs, with a consequent increase in self - criticism and isolation.

Healing Depression - How is Depression Treated? How can depression be cured?

In a 2018 study by Ijaz et al. Psychotherapy, added to traditional drug therapy (with antidepressants), has been highlighted to be beneficial for depressive symptoms and for short-term response and remission rates for patients with TRD (treatment-resistant depression). The medium- and long-term effects seem equally beneficial.

The Cognitive - Behavioral Therapy of depression is based on the combined use of behavioral and cognitive techniques. Considering the difficulties of attention, concentration, memory of the depressed subject , it is not advisable to intervene immediately on thoughts and emotions and consequently behavioral techniques are used first; as soon as the patient begins to engage in some purposeful constructive activity and there is, therefore, an improvement in mood and a modification of negative beliefs about their abilities and possibility of change, it is possible to start working more directly on the cognitive components through Technical specifications.

Healing from depression with behavioral techniques

The Behavioral Techniques are used above all in the first phase of the treatment and have the purpose of promoting BEHAVIORAL ACTIVATION. Depressive symptoms dramatically change people's lives, daily activities, and behavior. Many of these changes make the problem worse.

For example, lack of motivation or energy leads the depressed person to cut back on activities, neglect daily tasks and responsibilities, leaving others to make decisions often.

As we have already said, when you reduce your activities you tend to become less and less motivated, more tired and with less energy, triggering a vicious circle that thus determines a further worsening of the mood.

Deciding not to do the things you usually love to do anymore necessarily preclude the possibility of experiencing positive emotions and events.

Daily responsibilities and work tasks pile up because you don't have the strength to do them, and just thinking about this growing list of missed tasks can cause guilt or confirm your idea of being inadequate, unable or failed, making it even worse.

Depressive state.

One way to break this vicious circle is to increase your current level of activity, especially the pleasant ones. This makes it possible, in fact, to think of other things, not to ruminate and to look forward to regaining, so plan floor control of your again the pleasure to experience positive emotions.

We must not start by proposing to do too many activities all at once, because when you are depressed even the single actions that previously did not require any effort become a huge obstacle to overcome and seem to require a lot of energy.

Since thoughts such as "it's too hard", "I'll never make it", "I don't have the strength" or "I won't have fun doing it" might block, an initial goal might be to perform a task that requires little. Time.

Everyone will choose a task, even a small one, to start with.

Healing depression with cognitive techniques

Cognitive Techniques allow those suffering from depression to become aware of their thoughts and beliefs to learn how to modify them, thus managing their suffering.

The cornerstone of Cognitive - Behavioral Therapy of emotional disorders, and therefore also of depression, is: "The way you think affects the way you feel".

People, especially during episodes of intense depression, fail to understand that their thoughts influence their moods and that they play an important mediating function between the situation and the emotion with the consequent physiological reaction and between the situation. And behavior.

Let's see with a practical example how thoughts influence the state of mind.

Imagine being invited on a blind date.

Meetings this person in a room full of people and start talking, but he / she after introducing himself / a is limited to answer your questions without looking into his eyes and looking away.

Imagine the emotions you might feel if these three different thoughts occurred to you:

What a rude person! He doesn't even look at me while I talk to him / her! But why did he invite me!

Perhaps he is thinking that I am not interesting and that I am boring.

Maybe he's shy and doesn't look me in the eye.

Most likely these three thoughts of evaluating the behavior of the other described above are associated with three different emotional reactions. In the first case, for example, you will feel anger or frustration; in the second, disappointment and in the third hope.

Therefore, it is not the event itself that determines what you feel, but the way you interpret the situation through your thoughts.

In Cognitive - Behavioral Therapy there are two streams of thought, one of which we are most aware called *voluntary thoughts* , and others so fast and immediate that they are defined as " *automatic* ". Often, precisely because they are so fast, we do not have the awareness of the presence of automatic thoughts, but we have it more than the resulting emotions and the related physical sensations that accompany them.

The ABC model - a technique for identifying and monitoring automatic thoughts

Learning to recognize and change automatic dysfunctional thoughts can positively affect your mood. Typical negative automatic thoughts that run through the minds of depressed people are: "I'm a failure! I will never be able to do anything! I'm a fool", "They all consider me a fool and a loser, and they will surely leave me alone!"

ABC analysis is a technique for identifying and monitoring automatic thoughts.

A Triggering event

First you need to identify A that represents an event or situation in which you have experienced a strong negative emotion such as depression.

Point A describes the situation in the same way that a video camera would record it that is, telling only the facts, without reporting opinions and / or feelings.

A = Yesterday I was walking on the street and there were a lot of people around me. At one point I notice a friend of mine who is walking right in my direction, but when he comes close to me he does not greet me and passes by.

C Emotional and behavioral consequences

The next step is to identify C, which includes the emotions and behaviors that followed the event A. First, therefore, after identifying A, we need to identify the emotions felt in that situation and assign a score of intensity on a scale ranging from 0 to 100 (the higher the number the more intense the emotion). You can also write down the behaviors you adopted in that situation, such as going home immediately.

C = sadness 40%, disappointment 80%, upset 60%. I'll go home immediately

B your thoughts

At this point, the B's are identified, the thoughts that is what goes through your head at that moment.

B = - He saw me and didn't even say hello! - Surely he didn't want to talk to me and pretended not to see me - He must have thought he didn't want to waste time with a boring person like me!

After having identified A and C, therefore, to facilitate the identification of thoughts (B) we can ask ourselves: " What was I thinking when the event occurred?", "What was going through my mind?"

With the therapist's help, the patient learns to discuss the thoughts that cause one to experience negative emotion and to formulate alternative and more functional explanations (building a list as long as possible). This cognitive discussion has the function of helping the patient to distance himself from his thoughts and to begin to consider them as psychological events and not as data of reality.

HOW CAN YOU PREVENT DEPRESSION RELAPSE?

Preventing the relapse of depression

The depression is often a chronic condition that has some consequences that, although minor, interfere with normal daily activities and prevent the person to appreciate life and enjoy it fully.

Why Does Depression Return?

When people, for whatever reason, start thinking more negatively, depression reappears, because it is the thought that creates the emotion. During the first depressive episode, however, this negativity does not immediately emerge when the first thoughts are formulated, but it takes some time. After repeated depressive episodes, strong associations are formed and this means that even a small triggering stimulus, such as a normal mood decline, can be interpreted negatively and thus become a critical starting point for the reappearance of depression. From this critical point it triggers a spiral of thought ruminative negative that can progressively lead to a sense of hopelessness. Feeling hopeless then leads to social withdrawal and the avoidance of an increasing number of situations. Once the old thoughts are activated, often unconsciously, it is difficult to break free from the vicious circle that triggers a new depressive episode, because it is often the result of an instinctual reaction, just as it is to wriggle out of quicksand (Segal, Williams & Teasdale , 2013).

It is enormously important to remember that even when people feel well, the link between negative mood and thoughts negative remains ready to be reactivated. This implies, therefore, that in order to change one's attitude towards depression it is necessary to learn the strategies to prevent that, through rumination, one ends up again in a spiral out of control, even starting from a slight decrease in mood.

Preventing the relapse of depression with *Mindfulness-Based Cognitive Therapy (MBCT)*.

Studies by Zindel Segal (Toronto), Mark Williams (Wales) and John Teasdale (Cambridge) have given birth to the Mindfulness-Based Cognitive Therapy (MBCT) program. This protocol, which is a reworking of Jon Kabat-Zinn's work on the stress reduction program (MBSR) already tested on more than 24,000 patients over the past 20 years at the University of Massachusetts , investigated how meditation can help people to feel better after being successfully treated for depression. The work of Segal, Williams and Teasdale has been based on the observation that, once a patient has recovered from a depressive episode, a relatively small amount of negative mood, which can present itself, as we have said, for any reason, can re-trigger a great deal of classic negative thoughts of depression.

"I am a failure", "I am weak", "I am worthless", "I am hopeless" bring with them physical sensations of weakness, fatigue or inexplicable pain. Both negative thoughts and fatigue often seem disproportionate to the situation in the eyes of others.

Patients who believe they are cured may feel back to square one.

They find themselves in a ruminative loop that constantly leads them to ask themselves "what went wrong?", "Why is this happening to me?", "Where will all this take me?". Such rumination causes people to almost obsessively search for an answer, but in reality it only causes a prolongation and worsening of the depression. The MBCT protocol is designed to help those suffering from periods of chronic depression and unhappiness through a tool that allows them to deal with all of this when it recurs. The evidence for efficacy of MBCT is so robust that the *Anglo-Saxon National Institute for Clinical and Health Excellence (NICE)* recommends it to anyone who has had two or more depressive episodes.

In particular:

L ' MBCT is more effective maintenance doses of antidepressants in preventing relapse in depression

Three-quarters of those who took an MBCT course and took antidepressants were able to stop their medications within 15 months

L ' MBCT can reduce the severity of symptoms in individuals who are experiencing a depressive episode

L ' MBCT would seem to reduce the score to BDI (Beck Depression Inventory) in patients with drug resistant depression

The Mindfulness-Based Cognitive Therapy (MBCT) includes simple guided meditations that help participants to become more aware and able to accept this as well as it is, to get in touch with the changes of mind and body from moment to moment. The main purpose of an MBCT course is, as we have said, to help those who have suffered from depression in the past to learn skills that will help them prevent relapse in the future.

Recognize when the mood is about to subside

Become more aware of thoughts, emotions and physical sensations from moment to moment

Choose the most effective response to any unpleasant thoughts, feelings or situations you encounter

Develop a different way of relating to feelings, thoughts and emotions

Learning to consciously accept and recognize unwanted emotions and thoughts rather than going through habitual and automatic routines that tend to perpetuate difficulties

Find out what makes it more vulnerable to relapse and the activation of the vicious circles that determine the recurrence of the disorder

Blocking the escalation of negative thoughts and focusing on the present moment, rather than keeping an eye on the past or the future

To acquire a way of thinking and paying attention different from the usual one, without the automatic pilot

Preventing relapse with *Compassion Focused Therapy (CFT)*

The Compassion Focused Therapy (CFT) is a therapy developed by psychotherapist and researcher Paul Gilbert, professor of Clinical Psychology at the University Derby (UK) for many years studied human psychology from an evolutionary point of view. This approach integrates data from neuroscience and psychology with the teachings of the Buddhist tradition: *"if you want others to be happy, practice compassion; if you want to be happy yourself, practice compassion"* (Dalai Lama, 1995).

The Compassion Focused Therapy (CFT) is therefore a type of therapy that unfolds in the relationship between the psychotherapist and his patient: through the latter, in fact, the patient experienced in "the therapist's mind" the satisfaction of its need to be calmed and reassured. In this way the activation of the system focused on the threat is counteracted and the patient learns and builds, through this experience, new for him, his own safety system that will help him to regulate emotions and to remove feelings of shame and self-criticism.

The heart of CFT is represented by Compassionate Mind Training (CMT), composed of a set of techniques. Some of these are:

Writing compassionate letters to you;

Write compassionate thoughts on slips of paper that you always carry with you;

Listening to compassionate phrases spoken by the therapist and recorded on a tape;

Construction of compassionate images (e.g. "the perfect breeder") to be recalled when necessary;

Read your judgmental thoughts aloud as if listening to them were a friend in the same situation;

Giving a name to self and / or use the image of a person;

Three chair technique: one represents desires; the other represents duties and social standards interjected in conflict with desires. In the third (compassionate) chair the patient is seated and here he learns to empathize with both sides in conflict.

The aim is to encourage in the patient the construction of a non-judgmental and caring internal part and the expression and denomination of emotions, reading them adequately and in a non-interpretative way.

The goal of Compassion Focused Therapy (CFT) is not to change what a person feels (feel good), but the way they relate to what they feel (feel good), learning to tolerate their negative emotions and be with own suffering, caressing each other.

The question is very interesting because on this relationship there are completely discordant versions between them and each with a good amount of data to support it.

Having anxiety and depression at the same time is more serious than having just one

However the relationship between the two psychopathological forms is conceptualized, some data are confirmed.

Likelihood of having a greater number of relapses

Anderson's group noted that about 66% of adolescents diagnosed with anxiety will develop depressive disorder in the coming years.

Models regarding the anxiety-depression relationship

There are several models that evaluate the relationship between anxiety and depression.

According to some, anxiety and depression are the same phenomenon, as if to say that they are different parts of the same elephant. According to this orientation, one painting is the reflection of the other, one of the two components induces changes that make the other part emerge.

Other models view depression and anxiety as distinct entities but which share common factors. These could concern, for example, the type of stress, negative affectivity or certain type of vulnerability which, interacting with other parameters, determines the emergence of the pathology.

Still other models view depression and anxiety as two distinct and separate entities that share absolutely nothing. Thus in the same subject we accidentally observe two paintings that share only temporality. As if to say that a subject suffers in the same day from toothache and knee pain without any link between the two phenomena.

A critical examination

Let's try to examine some of the points mentioned above.

A factor that actually seems to unite anxiety and depression is the presence, in both situations, of negative affectivity. In particular, feeling irritable and not very sensitive to activities usually considered pleasant.

Negative affectivity we find feelings like anger, the guilt, the shame, the sadness, the disgust, the concern, the feeling contemptuous.

An argument that leads to differentiate the two pictures distinguishes two constructs: positive affectivity and neurovegetative hyper-activation (arousal). Starting from this distinction, low levels of positive affect and high levels of negative affect are noted in the depressed subject. On the contrary, anxious subjects would show high levels of arousal and negative affectivity but not necessarily reduction of positive affectivity.

In the clinical setting, the absence of positive affect is revealed by the use of terms such as fatigue, tiredness, and slowdown. The increased arousal is expressed instead with references to the sense of somatic tension, shortness of breath, sweating, dizziness or dizziness, dry mouth.

The weakness of this construct is the observation that in anxious subjects the appreciable autonomic symptoms are mostly present in panic disorder, not necessarily in all forms of anxiety.

Role of genetics

Data from genetics studies seem to support all theories. Most studies agree that family history is the most correlated factor in the co-presence of anxiety and depression.

In other studies, relatives of subjects with anxiety and depression were more likely to suffer from unipolar depression, alcoholism but not anxiety spectrum disorders.

Those with depression and generalized anxiety disorder (GAD) had twice as many relatives with depression as those with depression alone or GAD alone.

Some studies have found genetic elements that unite the two disorders: children of people with depression or anxiety were more likely to develop both a depressive and anxious disorder.

Neurobiology of anxiety and depression

Alterations have been reported in the central nervous system that is common to anxiety and depression, particularly in circuits in component serotonergic,dopaminergic, noradrenergic and GABAergic.

Prolonged activation of the centers that generate arousal could over time lead to depletion of neurotransmitters that would cause depressive disorders.

It appears that anomalies concerning estradiol are common to the two disorders, as well as modifications of the corticotrophin releasing hormone (GRH). The latter figure that seems to unite the two disorders is however in contrast with other results. The increased production of CRH was found in both disorders. However, while depressed subjects show an abnormality of the parameters of the hypothalamic-pituitary axis at baseline, this is not observed in patients with GAD.

Pharmacological and psychological therapies

We have long known that drug treatment with antidepressants improves both depressive disorders and anxiety disorders. Many of these molecules in fact report in the technical data sheet the indication for both disorders.

This would confirm the hypothesis of a biological factor that unites the two disorders. But in clinical experience we know that this is not the case: there are situations in which the treatment of depression with antidepressants leads to the onset of anxiety symptoms or the exacerbation of these.

On the other hand, anxiolytic therapies do not improve depressive symptoms; on the contrary they often worsen them by accentuating asthenia, cognitive difficulties or affective flattening.

The psychotherapy: Cognitive Behavioral has shown a great therapeutic tool either alone that as a support to drug treatment. On the other hand, these patients are difficult to treat pharmacologically due to hyper vigilance and hypersensitivity to even minimal side effects.

The cognitive and behavioral psychotherapy is able to be able to have as therapeutic targets both depressive symptoms that anxious for example through interventions of motivation, reevaluation of cognitive distortions, interventions on cognitive schemes, improvements in self-regulation and training of social skills .

I believe that convincing clarifications on the anxiety-depression relationship will not arrive any time soon for many reasons. The principal, in my opinion, is that terms such as anxiety and depression do not want to say anything; I personally regard these terms as a doctor considers the word "fever".

There are many forms of anxiety and as many forms of depression: if we then imagine combining the many components, such a large number of combinations would emerge as to make any sensible evaluation impossible.

To this we must add many other components that characterize the complexity of man: temperamental factors, the intellectual level, the history of development and the history of life, environmental factors and much more.

This does not mean that it is always very useful to stop and reflect on the state of the art of research, keeping our mental elasticity active, an excellent antidote to dogmatism that is sometimes present even among professionals.

ANXIETY IN RELATIONSHIP

Relationship Anxiety: How to Deal with It in the Couple

It's not just the fear of commitment itself, but also the stress and worry that manifest at any stage of the relationship.

It is the doubts, the few certainties, the triggering of thoughts that arise even in situations where things do not necessarily go wrong.

This anxiety can actually hinder the feeling and the relationship, it is often an anticipatory anxiety, but it can be reduced through several ways.

Relationship anxiety: what are they?

So many things and situations can cause relationship anxiety in couples, and they often differ depending on how the relationship was born and developed.

The anxieties that arise from situations of "violent relationships " are different from anxieties that develop as a result of raising children.

Some people suffer from anxiety regardless of the relationship with the other and when they establish a relationship they bring this difficulty with them.

This is a very broad subject; so many books have been written on how and why some people develop anxiety in a relationship.

Some of these behaviors include:

Aggressive language

Hiding things (like being vague, not warning of a delay, etc.)

In other cases, anxiety can come from reasons unrelated to the partner's behavior, such as fear of abandonment.

Or some people feel anxious because their partner is "too much into something": too rich, too beautiful, too busy, too outgoing, and so on. In this case the partner has qualities that "lead to anxiety ".

Correctly assessing the quality of the relationship is crucial in determining how to eliminate anxiety.

It can also cause discomfort to the other person who doesn't know how to deal with the problem or wants to fight it together with their partner.

Relating to those who suffer from anxiety can be more difficult especially when you do not have the tools to overcome this state.

It is also true that it depends a lot on what kind of anxiety, how intense and how often the partner suffers.

The relationship itself causes anxiety

For many people, however, the question of anxiety can be asked about the quality and experience of the relationship itself.

It isn't necessarily a single partner behavior or a general fear of commitment.

Sometimes, anxiety comes progressively over time, caused by a number of different factors regardless of whether you are in a happy or unhappy relationship.

There can be very serious and less serious problems that cause anxiety. In any case, when you find yourself anxious during a relationship it is always very complicated because the relationship itself suffers.

This can in turn be caused by the many discussions, by previous breakups or it can come from much further away.

In this case, for some, the uncertainty of the relationship risks becoming an uncertainty of life and future projects.

Trust is a very important element of a serious relationship, and if it is lacking, it is very difficult to regain it naturally.

Too many discussions

Having too much discussion is often a problem. It is clear that it depends a lot on the tone, the type and the ego that comes out of it.

But the problem isn't just that arguments can involve anger.

There is also concern that these discussions may be repeated several times in the future.

This worry can cause a lot of anxiety, because you risk being afraid to do anything, perhaps at home or in other shared situations, because you are worried about repeating other discussions at any time.

Negativity

In relationships where there are a lot of arguments it is possible there is also a lot more negativity.

It may be that the relationship of one to the other, or even of one of the two, is no longer as friendly and supportive as it was at the beginning of the relationship.

Even funny things risk becoming negative situations and often things said in disagreement are expressed with a hostile tone and not one of improvement / growth of the relationship.

The constant negativity risks causing anxiety in the couple.

Stress

Of course, perhaps the most common general reason in a relationship where anxiety is present is the prolonged presence of stress.

Stress becomes the cause of anxiety in a medium to long period.

This may have been due to the situation within the couple, such as external situations of high stress (work, family, friends, etc.).

How does anxiety manifest itself in a romantic relationship?

The above are just the general causes of anxiety in a relationship and clearly cannot cover every single case.

Often people then begin to have the same more common symptoms of anxiety, such as:

- o Agitation / nervousness
- o Insomnia
- o Muscle tension
- o Feelings of depression
- o Sweating

Very often the anxiety that is created in the relationship also flows into other areas of the person's life.

Reason why it is no longer a relationship anxiety, but can easily be considered as an anxiety disorder caused by a troubled relationship.

In this case you may want to consider supplementing your diet with some natural anxiolytics such as theanine, GABA or lavender.

Relationship anxiety: what cure?

Two questions to ask

Relationships today are very complicated.

It sounds paradoxical, but breakups are actually an important part of relationships.

If the ideal goal is to be with a person who makes you feel good and happy, maybe the person you have a long-lasting relationship with anxiety may not be the right person for you.

The second question is based on a simple truth about relationships: you can only change yourself.

Despite your commitment to trying to "sensitize" your partner to a change, you can't be the one to change it. Only your partner can change.

Your role therefore is to try to be the best partner possible and as open as possible, with the (subjective) hope that your partner will be more motivated accordingly to change what is wrong and subsequently create anxiety.

Relationship anxiety: how to get out of it

Overcoming the anxiety in the couple involves a reflection on the causes and on what can be changed.

It is advisable to have a clear and calm mind before starting to deal with the arguments, so first of all it is important to reduce stress and anxiety in general.

The ways in which the problems will be addressed will certainly be a fundamental element for the success or failure of the reduction of anxiety in relationships.

Let's now see what the possible remedies for couple anxiety are:

1. *Physical activity and other strategies to combat anxiety*

Anxiety in the couple is still anxiety, so it is important to use the most common techniques to decrease anxiety.

The most recommended is certainly physical activity. It's easy to integrate into everyone's life, and exercise is just as powerful as most anxiety-fighting drugs.

2. *Start over*

If trust fails, it is important to talk to your partner to think about starting all over again. Trust is essential, and to build it needs to start from the bottom.
If after a few weeks things are improving, it is still too early to say that confidence has returned.
After that it is not going to take much longer to regain it.

3. *Comparison on the needs of each one*

Try to talk to your partner about each other's needs. Write down a list of things that are important and try to do them, as long as it doesn't go against each other's morals.

Not all the written things are done, but it's important to try to be the best partner you can. It is possible to find that your partner is also motivated to improve.

If you don't see any improvement after a month, your partner may not have an interest in satisfying some of your needs.

4. *Stay mentally busy*

Keeping your mind busy with other things can be difficult if you suffer from anxiety during a relationship. But this detachment can help you improve your mood.

Often the mind is our enemy and needs to be directed away from thoughts related to your love life.

Look for distractions like outdoor activities, watching TV, spending time with animals, hanging out with friends, and so on.

5. *Show affection physically*

Seek physical contact with your partner, even just holding hands can be relaxing at times.

Many couples that last for many years often hug after a long day at work. Trying to be more affectionate can send your partner a signal of closeness.

ANXIETY IN SOCIAL RELATIONSHIPS

The Social Phobia or Social Anxiety Disorder is an anxiety disorder, in which the characteristic fear is the belief of being watched and judged negatively in social situations or when carrying out an activity in public . What is mainly feared is the negative judgment of others. Generally, people with this disorder fear, in social and otherwise unfamiliar situations, that they will be able to say or do embarrassing things and to be judged anxious, awkward, stupid, incompetent, strange, clumsy, weak or "crazy".

The person with the disorder generally has this fear when talking to others, when he does or says something while others are watching him or even if there is simply the possibility of attracting the attention of others; for example, he is afraid of being misjudged by others if they realize he is anxious (blushes, sweats, trembles). Or are you afraid to say or do something wrong or embarrassing, appear clumsy, or have a panic attack (eg. Often have thoughts like ".... Now clumsy will appear, clumsy ... I will start to shake and sweat ... the others will notice and they will laugh at me! ") . Still others may feel anxious that others may find them unpleasant and / or criticize their appearance.

Generally the most commonly feared situations are: speaking in public, going to a party, writing or signing in front of someone, queuing up, using the telephone in public, using public transport. Some people fear, for example, of having embarrassing physiological reactions (e.g. losing bladder control, throwing up, burping, etc.) and some are more afraid of situations in which they are asked for a performance, others, instead, of occasions for social interaction: typical examples of this last case are expressed in situations in which the person affected by the disorder fears that he has nothing to say or say something wrong, that he will be boring or, in any case, inadequate.

These fears may be present only in some social situations (specific social phobia) or in the majority of them (generalized social phobia). In any case, the person suffering from social phobia faces such situations with extreme discomfort and anxiety, so often, in order not to experience such unpleasant sensations, he will begin to avoid the feared social situations in every way, with the idea that he will be well by avoiding exposure to them. The reasons for avoidance can be different: you may feel an anxiety so intense that it is unmanageable or you may be tired of facing situations in which you struggle with your feeling of inadequacy. In some cases, avoidances can lead to the person's social isolation.

The so-called "anticipatory anxiety" is also typical : anxiety in itself has a developmentally "anticipatory" function, in the sense that it is an emotional signal that warns us, in terms of forecasting hypotheses, that our purpose could be compromised; in fact, before facing a feared event (e.g. a student who has to take an exam) a person may feel anxiety because in advance he repeatedly imagines the occurrence of that event, perhaps with images of himself in which he will make a bad impression, will be awkward, it will look stupid. Images of what is feared may show up for days before having to deal with the feared event, thus increasing the level of anxiety. On some occasions, the anxiety can become so intense that it actually hinders the subject in carrying out his tasks. During a meeting, for example, he may be so anxious that he is very unclear in presenting concepts.

Therefore, those suffering from social phobia, when they have a very high level of anxiety, can really have poor performance. The realization of what you fear most usually causes further embarrassment, shame, or a sense of humiliation. A vicious circle can thus be established that feeds the disorder over time, as it maintains the fear of negative judgment and anticipatory anxiety over time.

Another condition that is usually associated with "avoidance" behaviors is represented by the so-called "protective " behaviors. These are the "safety measures" that the person takes to prevent anxiety or being misjudged by others. For example, if the person is at a business meeting and feels ashamed because if he takes off his jacket you will notice that he is sweating, in which case he will keep the jacket on and this protective behavior, paradoxically, will only increase sweating and therefore, consequently, the embarrassment, creating a vicious circle. So, the problems emotions are most frequent in social phobia have anxiety / fear , the ' embarrassment , the shame and humiliation; when the person is in this particular state of mind and mood it is even more likely that he has images of disapproval, derision, rejection or pain of others, feeling, at times, a true terror. The fear of being judged negatively can sometimes be so strong that it is accompanied by obvious symptoms of anxiety: palpitations, tremors in the hands or legs, sweating, gastrointestinal discomfort, diarrhea, muscle tension, confusion. In the most serious cases, the fear of negative judgment can cause real panic attacks. Anxious symptoms are often associated with typical reactions of shame: flushing of the face, modest posture, and desire to escape the gaze of others or to "sink".

The following are the specific symptoms of social phobia or Social Anxiety Disorder that define the disorder:

Marked fear or anxiety about one or more social situations in which the individual is exposed to the possible judgment of others

This disorder is quite common: scientific studies indicate that in Europe, for example, it affects an average of 2.3% of the general population. Since social phobia sufferers are unlikely to seek help from specialists because they underestimate their problem or are ashamed of it, it is likely that this disorder is even more widespread than research suggests. Social phobia generally appears more or less abruptly in adolescence, around the age of 15, after a childhood characterized by inhibition and shyness. Later it tends to remain over time, with variations in severity linked to life events.

How to tell if you have social phobia

To understand if you suffer from the disorder, it is necessary to make a fundamental clarification, which also applies to all other emotional situations, so that they are not always considered problematic. Anticipatory anxiety, embarrassment, shame, a sense of humiliation, fear of being judged negatively, and fear of being ashamed are emotions that anyone can experience. However, this condition does not always represent a purely clinical problem, as it could simply be simple shyness, certainly a cause of discomfort, but not limiting for the person's life if it does not turn into anxiety disorder. So how is a social phobia disorder different from a condition of simple shyness or from a physiological emotional reaction? In people who suffer from a social phobia, first of all, emotional states are so intense and debilitating that hinders the normal course of daily life. People who do not suffer from Social Phobia generally begin to worry only shortly before the situation begins, usually during the situation they become less shy and anxious, so much so that, the following times, they will tend to worry less about it. The anxiety is therefore not overwhelming; it disappears quickly during or immediately after the end of the situation and does not lead the person to avoid it the following times. Those suffering from Social Phobia , on the other hand, tend to worry long before the event to be faced; he is always worse off when he is in the feared situation; the next time he may be even more worried than the previous one, so he may engage in avoidance and / or protective behaviors . So, if what we define shyness or discomfort leads the person to avoid social encounters or in any case causes very intense anxiety in social situations, and then we speak of a real Social Phobia.

This disorder is very disabling for the person affected, as it significantly limits the habits of a person, compromising, in a more or less serious way, even the very autonomy, social functioning, school and / or work. As a result, often, this condition will also affect mood, due to the frustration of seeing one's life limited. Therefore, Social Phobia lasts a long time, it could generate intense sadness and mood swings as the person evaluates how much their life has changed since the onset of the disorder and often feels feelings of loss of hope about possible solutions.

To obtain a serious and accurate diagnosis, however, it is necessary to contact qualified people.

Another condition to keep in mind, for the purpose of a correct diagnosis, is that many of the symptoms present in Social Phobia are also common to other psychological disorders. For example, the person with Social Phobia may have panic attacks like those suffering from Panic Disorder , however the latter tends to have them in situations that are not necessarily social ones, unlike those who experience them only in social situations (Social Phobia); moreover, those with Panic Disorder usually avoid being alone because they feel the presence of other people as reassuring; the person suffering from Social Phobia, on the other hand, seeks loneliness because it is precisely the social situations that cause him discomfort.

Social phobia can also be confused with Generalized Anxiety Disorder. The two disorders, in fact, have in common the fear of feeling embarrassed or humiliated, but in Generalized Anxiety Disorder this fear is not the main concern of the individual, as it happens in Social Phobia. Furthermore, subjects with generalized anxiety worry about the quality of their performance continuously, even when they are not judged, while in Social Phobia the main reason that triggers the anxiety is the judgment of others. The scarcity of social relations characterized by both social phobia that the schizoid personality disorder. In the latter, however, loneliness is a consequence of the lack of interest in social relationships, while in social phobia it is a consequence of social avoidances. The social phobic, in fact, feels interest in other people, has the desire to have social relationships and feels anguish because of his socialization difficulties. Social phobia has several characteristics in common with avoidant personality disorder as well. In both cases, the person presents avoidance of social situations, low self-esteem and extreme sensitivity to negative judgments. The two disorders, however, seem to differ in that the person with avoidant disorder has a pervasive fear in all social and relational situations, while those suffering from social phobia have fears more specifically related to social performance, so if they have to expose themselves to do a task in public. This distinction, however, does not make it easy to differentiate between avoidant personality disorder and generalized social phobia. According to some experts, in fact, these two diagnoses would be super imposable, in other words it would be possible that two different diagnostic categories are being used for the same disorder. Other authors, however, argue that there are differences between these two pathologies. From the results of a research, in fact, it appears that people with avoidant personality disorder, compared to those with generalized social phobia, have greater interpersonal sensitivity and poorer social skills. According to other authors, moreover, the two disorders would be distinguishable on the basis of what activates the sense of inadequacy and anxiety: subjects with social phobia usually feel inadequate when they have to perform services in the eyes of other people, while those with avoidant disorder are perceived inadequate especially when, in relating to others, they feel a strong sense of extraneousness and non-belonging.

 Finally, the presence of social phobia is excluded if social anxiety and avoidance occur in the course of other mental disorders that may justify them (e.g. depression) or in conjunction with concerns relating to a medical condition (e.g. tremor in Parkinson's, scars).

Causes of social phobia

According to recent studies there is no single cause of social phobia: a set of factors contribute to the onset of the disorder, which can be genetic, psychological and environmental. As for the genetic factors, they would correspond to a tendency to have anxious reactions more easily, connected to a greater reactivity and sensitivity of the nervous system. First of all, a familiarity with the development of social phobia was found: compared to the rest of the population, in fact the probability of developing Social Phobia is higher in the close relatives of those who suffer from it. Another risk factor is the presence of some personality characteristics (psychological factors), whose development is affected, once again, by genetic, environmental and educational factors. By personality we mean the habitual way of thinking, reacting and relating to others. The most frequently reported by the same descriptions of people with social phobia personality traits are usually the sensitivity to criticism and opinions of others and the refusal, the tendency to have emotional reactions, easy to concerns often are concerned about having to make a good impression of oneself to others, the feeling of being weak, difficulties in being assertive, low self-esteem and the feeling of inferiority. Among the environmental risk factors finally, they consider the experiences in which the person has felt humiliated or ridiculed and high stress levels associated with major life changes (e.g. Work assignments that require public speaking, partner loss); even the family education received can contribute positively to increasing self-confidence and favoring interpersonal relationships, or negatively by strengthening social fears.

Consequences of social phobia

This disorder causes a significant impairment of the quality of life in general, in particular in a number of important areas of life such as the workplace, school, social and affective.

Academic difficulties are often caused by the presence of performance anxiety. Problems in the workplace, on the other hand, are more often caused by the fear of public speaking and the tendency to avoid commitments in which the person might feel negatively valued, such as doing jobs in contact with the public. In severe cases these difficulties can lead to dropping out of school or work, or lead to a state unemployment due to ' avoidance of discussions of work. From the point of view of social and emotional, individuals with this diagnosis are less likely to have social and romantic relationships than the general population. In severe cases, the person can isolate himself completely. These difficulties can also contribute to the development of feelings of frustration, sadness and a sense of dissatisfaction with oneself and for one's life, or a depressive disorder, or even drug abuse as an attempt to alleviate suffering. Such secondary situations further complicate the described picture.

Different types of treatment

In recent years, various studies have been carried out on the effectiveness of psychotherapies for the treatment of social phobia. Studies show that the therapies that are effective for treating this disorder are behavioral therapy, Social Skill Training groups and cognitive-behavioral therapy.

The behavioral therapy is a treatment focused on the technique of 'gradual exposure, which involves gradually exposing the patient to the feared situation so that it can reduce social anxiety and gain a sense of effectiveness in the management of social situations.

The social skills training (link group phobic), or training for social skills, is a group treatment aimed at the development or increase of social skills (e.g. The ability of conflict resolution) and the acquisition of personal mode deal with feared interpersonal situations. In a "protected" environment, the patient may be able to change the representation of himself by experimenting with social relationships with other members of the group and using feedback on his own behavior.

Those suffering from social phobia can also benefit from a drug treatment based on new generation antidepressants and benzodiazepines.

Pharmacotherapy is often used to create favorable conditions for more effective psychotherapeutic intervention. For this reason, the clinician often proposes to the patient an intervention in which pharmacological and psychotherapeutic treatment are combined. Generally the pharmacological treatment alone is not effective, as the interruption of the pharmacotherapy, the symptoms recur. Drugs, in fact, in a relatively short time reduce the intensity of the symptoms that characterize the disorder, but do not resolve the "causes" underlying the disorder; in essence it would be like treating a strong making exclusive use of painkillers back pain: it is likely that after some time, the pain will recur unless it also acts on what it has caused. In fact, drugs, in the case of Social Phobia, by lowering the levels of subjective suffering and anxiety, are used in an initial phase of treatment as they create the favorable conditions for an effective psychotherapeutic intervention (to be understood, if a person is very agitated it will be difficult for him to have sufficient concentration and "lucidity" to allow him to "learn" or follow a psychotherapy session).

For these reasons, the patient is often advised to follow both a pharmacological treatment (limited in time as much as possible) and a psychotherapeutic one.

In fact, drug therapy does not always is prescribed, but it is necessary at least temporarily, for people who have very intense activation anxious. A condition that often arises as an obstacle to taking drugs of this type is the "fear", sometimes conviction, of developing an addiction to these drugs; often this is a prejudice that hinders the effectiveness of the treatment. Indeed, some drugs (e.g. benzodiazepines) can cause addiction in the long term, however taking the drug under the supervision of an expert doctor (psychiatrist) avoids and decreases the risk of this condition.

The cognitive-behavioral treatment

Scientific research claims that cognitive-behavioral therapy is one of the most effective treatments for social phobia. The cognitive-behavioral protocol for the treatment of this disorder involves the use of the following procedures:

Formulation of a therapeutic contract, which contains shared objectives between patient and therapist and their respective tasks (e.g. homework for the patient);

Reconstruction of the history of the disorder , starting from the first episode in which it occurred, up to the detailed description of the current manifestation;

Formulation of the functioning scheme of the disorder, starting from the analysis of recent episodes during which the person has experienced social anxiety;

Interventions type psychoeducational, which provides information on the nature of the anxiety and shame and their role in the onset and maintenance of the disorder;

Identification of the dysfunctional thoughts underlying the disorder and questioning of these interpretations through specific techniques (e.g. behavioral experiments, Socratic dialogue);

Learning techniques for managing anxiety symptoms (e.g. slow breathing technique, isometric and progressive muscle relaxation, etc.);

Gradual exposure to feared and avoided thoughts and stimuli, through the use of specific techniques (e.g. imaginative, interceptive and in vivo exposure);

At the end of the treatment, relapse prevention interventions.

This protocol is applicable both individually and in groups. In the case of social phobia, group treatment constitutes in itself an exposure to what the subject fears, so it must be implemented following the patient's preparation for it. It is also possible to carry out this therapy protocol in groups. The group therapy with respect to that individual has the general advantage of enabling the comparison with other people who are suffering from the same disorder and to favor, so, the scaling of the problem and the reduction of the sensation of subjective be "abnormal". Regarding the exposures (effective exercises to desensitization to the stimulus anxiety-inducing), are provided, where proves necessary, home visits at an early stage, in such a way as to support the person to start to be exposed, in order to then be able to continue alone.

Anxiety and worry about work. What to do? 9 tips to follow

The theme of work is often at the center of many of our concerns because it involves our present and future practical life but also many aspects of the self that play a fundamental role in our well-being. Among the most frequent concerns linked to the current trend of the labor market we find that of being able to lose one's job, with the consequent concern of not being able to find another one, or of finding one of a lower level or with lower pay. Then there is the concern linked to technological advancement which always makes us a step behind those who are younger than us and which forces us to review our skills which risk becoming obsolete. There is the concern linked to a socio-cultural factor according to which one must retire with the company where one entered the world of work. This is what happened in the past and that often the family culture has passed on to us, but we know it is an extremely unlikely event nowadays.

Then there are a series of concerns that instead have to do with our personality style, with our values, with our beliefs about work, with how much we identify with what we do and how much our self-esteem depends on the results. Working hours obtained. So we often end up worrying about doing our job perfectly, receiving criticism from our boss, being able to lose our job and consequently feel bankrupt and mulling over a lot of time about how terribly unfair this is.

Whatever exactly our particular concern with work is, it always stems from some general factors briefly described below:

Imposter Syndrome: Described by psychologists Harvey and Katz, it consists in thinking that you have somehow induced others to overestimate your worth and abilities. On the contrary, one's worth or success is attributed to ease of work or luck. Hence the fear of being discovered by others or being exposed just like an impostor. The felt insecurity negatively affects the work performance which inevitably tends to worsen.

Need to be appreciated and judged fairly: often in the workplace we seek the gratification of personal needs such as to be treated fairly, to be appreciated for the work done and possibly rewarded. However, if our vision of work is based on these needs, any criticism from the boss or any lack of approval will make us frustrated and resentful. Resentment will increase the feeling that we are not achieving our goals and that this is because of the boss or colleagues who do not recognize our competence. The anxious brooding and negative emotion experienced will lead us to worry even more about our future work. Furthermore, negative thoughts could generalize, leading us to think that there is no justice in the world of work and that things are not going as they should. Such thoughts could consequently lead us to carry out passive aggressive behaviors such as postponing the work to be done or doing it in an inaccurate way, through which to express our disappointment. The negative effect, however, is to create additional worries about the possibility that the boss will notice and criticize us or, in the worst case, fire us.

Perfectionism: refers to the fear of not being able to do one's job better, a fear that often drives us to work many hours longer than normal hours and to neglect a whole series of extra-work commitments such as family, friends, sport etc. The risk is to invest all our time in work, worsening the quality of family and interpersonal relationships by cutting off the possibility of obtaining gratifications from them. By restricting our interest only to work, we will also increase concerns about it. If the gratifications from work are scarce, a burn-out syndrome could develop, which in addition to worsening our psychophysical health will make us feel bankrupt even in the only field in which we have invested all our resources.

Overwork: it is now a proven fact that in the last twenty years the annual working hours have increased compared to the past, partly due to the desire to grow and have a career, partly due to economic necessity. In fact, the increased investment of people in the workplace does not find the same type of increased commitment of companies towards it. In fact, this commitment does not always correspond to the desired results, but on the contrary, sometimes the job is lost due to company mergers, staff reduction, etc.

Decline of the sense of community: by sense of community we mean the sense of constant collaboration between individuals aimed at achieving common goals, values or activities. The absence of participation in a community in which to feel part of outside the work context can make us more vulnerable. Both because we lack a support that can help us in moments of work difficulty, and because it can generate in us the belief that our personal needs can only be satisfied by work.

What to do?

Some tips to follow to start doing something about our concerns can be the following:

1- First of all ask yourself questions about when you need to worry and when not. In this way we will be able to discover our "theory" of worry. That is, we will find the reasons why we think it is useful to worry. For example, many people find that thinking about a problem for a long time is an effective way to find a solution.

2- Then focus on when it is useful and when not to worry about work. Thus, for example, we will be able to distinguish between concerns about an unknown and distant future and those about the present, thus focusing our attention on the situations in which we can intervene today and thus evaluate how. By contrasting our concerns in a concrete and finalized way, we will be able to deny the negative beliefs that supported our malaise.

3- Accept reality for what it is without opposing change. Some of the realities that people refuse to accept are in most cases: uncertainty and injustice. Perceiving a situation as uncertain or unfair causes in many people feelings of anxiety or anger that are difficult to manage that are faced by stubbornly trying to oppose the event that caused them even when this behavior proves not useful or even counterproductive.

4- Begin to think about your way of thinking and relate it to your malaise. Often, in fact, it is not so much the situation itself that is particularly negative and makes us feel bad, but the meaning that we attribute to it and therefore the type of thoughts and reasoning with which we evaluate it.

5- Ask yourself what the deepest perceived threat is . What are the basic beliefs that conflict with the situation we are experiencing? Once these beliefs have been identified, we will have the opportunity to question them, to understand where they originate from and how much they are currently useful to us or how much on the contrary they can be reviewed and modified with a view to well-being and functionality.

6- Downsizing the fear of criticism and failure. In the case of concern for work it is important to focus on the positive, on our behaviors that have a good chance of success and create alternatives to one's current job, taking into account our aspirations but also the reality of the labor market.

7- It is also important to develop a good sense of belonging to the community , to invest in one's interpersonal relationships, on participation in activities of collective interest that allow us to experience a feeling of belonging outside the work and to satisfy otherwise unfulfilled personal needs.

8- Use the emotions felt, as a signal to better understand what is happening to us, as feedback from which to draw suggestions on decisions or behaviors to be implemented. Don't use them as a cause of your worries. Dealing with your emotions gives you the opportunity to discover deep values and beliefs that guide us and then possibly revise them in the event that they no longer prove to be functional for us.

9- Dedicate yourself to the present moment, establish activities to carry out when you happen to worry, that do not have to do with work. Engaging in pleasant or sporting activities, for example, helps to detach the mind from one's anxieties and to experience positive emotions. Other activities such as yoga, meditative activities or breathing exercises can help us to live our emotions more peacefully and to manage them in a functional way.

It is clear that depending on the intensity of the anxiety experienced and the consequent difficulties in thinking or acting, it can be difficult to face the situation alone. The same objective can then be pursued through the support of a psychotherapist psychologist. The specialist will be able to provide first of all support and understanding regarding the problem, he will frame it in order to understand what factors keep it preventing us from overcoming it on our own. Together with you, he will establish the most suitable therapeutic path for the case.

ANXIETY ATTACK

"The subterfuges of hope are as ineffective as the arguments of reason" (Cioran, 1993) when the heart beats wildly, the breath becomes labored, the body seems to be crossed by a high voltage electric current and the mind runs fast, looking of a solution to those feelings that one cannot explain. The need for help and protection, as well as the attempt to escape from that situation that you only want it to stop, impede any attempt to control yourself and your reactions. Then, suddenly, everything ends, leaving the same feeling of devastation produced by a tsunami, in this psychological case. Until the next time. We have just taken a walk in crippling fear; the one that terrifies, the one that annihilates. But how can it happen that from a natural fear it is possible to structure a real disorder, from which the person cannot get rid of? Fear, as our endowment of nature, comes before and after everything, pushing us to act in anticipation of the same mind, with speed and precision. At the same time, precisely because of the characteristics described, when it attacks us it destroys all the rest and reason is shipwrecked, fear surpasses itself and becomes a limitation from a great resource; becomes panic.

Panic understood as a psychological disorder is a modern diagnostic category, although the characteristic reaction as a response to conditions of extreme threat, or the so-called "fear panic", is the most archaic of emotions. The WHO (World Health Organization), in 2000, defined panic disorder as the most important existing disease, affecting 20% of the population. From a nosographic perspective, in the DSM (Diagnostic and Statistical Manual of Mental Disorders), panic attacks have been contradictorily included within the category of anxiety disorders.

While, from an operational point of view, it appears that it is not anxiety that triggers fear, but it is fear that triggers the physiological reaction of anxiety, which increases more and more with the rise of the perception of individual threat, transforming itself thus from functional loss of control activation mechanism. Following this logic, if the activation of anxiety is an effect of the perception of stimuli internal or external to the organism, the privileged ways of treatment become the management and transformation of perceptions that activate the reactions of the subject in moments of crisis, while the classification of panic attacks among anxiety disorders leads to a distortion of observation and evaluation of the disorder, indicating as the most adequate solution the drug inhibitory therapy of anxiety itself. It is no coincidence that the first false positive in the diagnosis of panic is represented precisely by generalized anxiety disorder, where in reality the total loss of control typical of panic is missing; the state of alarm is constant, with an increase in physiological parameters, which however do not reach the tilt.

From the etiological point of view, although the really rigorous methodology to understand how pathology works is represented by the type of therapeutic solution capable of solving it, most of the time the perspective remains the traditional one that searches in the past for the causes of the present problem. However, during a panic attack, the person is terrified of his own feelings of fear towards the threatening stimulus he will try to fight, as we will see, thus increasing them; the effect therefore becomes cause. Therapeutic change can only take place within the present dynamics of persistence of the problem, thus acting on the way in which the individual perceives threatening stimuli and, reacting to them, instead of managing them functionally, is overwhelmed. The focus of the study is the interaction of the organism with its reality, to which it responds by modifying it and being modified by it. Panic is defined by many as the most extreme form of fear which, if below a certain threshold represents a resource that allows the organism to be alerted to dangerous situations, above this limit it becomes pathological. There are different situations in which the thrill of fear envelops the person in its coils, but the operating structure of the vicious circle that creates and maintains the fear itself is similar, until it becomes panic.

Analyzing the most usual reactions to a perception of intense fear, we can observe some constant redundancies in different people and situations:

a) The attempt to avoid or shy away from what frightens, which makes one feel less and less capable of facing that monster that takes on increasingly gigantic proportions in the mind of those who are afraid

b) The search for help and protection, which makes them feel save, but then, even if we succeed, it will be just a buffer that will take effect until the next time. This is because a sort of delegation to the other takes place in facing the fear which, being an individual perception, can be exorcised only and only by those who feel it;

c) The unsuccessful attempt to keep one's physiological reactions under control, which paradoxically causes one to lose control, for which one agitates even more.

The recurrence of this type of interaction over time increases the perception of fear leading to an exasperation of the physiological parameters that are activated naturally in the presence of threatening stimuli, up to the outbreak of panic. If, on the contrary, one manages to interrupt these dysfunctional interactions, fear falls within the limits of functionality (Nardone, 1993, 2000, 2003). The latter claim was precisely the hypothesis from which Giorgio Nardone and associates, have taken the first steps for the development of specific protocols of intervention: the ' avoidance, the request for help and the attempt to control bankruptcy are really what turns a fear reaction into panic, then making a person suffering from this disorder stop such response scripts should lead to the extinction of the disorder. In 1987 the first application of a specific therapeutic protocol for panic attacks with agoraphobia was carried out, based on a strategic sequence of therapeutic stratagems that created the planned random events, which led the subjects first to experience the corrective emotional experience, to then be exposed gradually to feared situations, touching hands with the new skills acquired.

The first research-intervention published in 1988 (Nardone, 1988) represented the milestone of all the work on panic developed in the following decades to date, demonstrating its extraordinary effectiveness and therapeutic efficiency in breaking the rigidity of the phobic perceptive-reactive system. Obsessive dysfunctional. Currently , the therapeutic treatment developed, and thus tested and proven, represents the "best practice " in the therapy of panic attacks, responding to all the criteria established in order to evaluate, from an epistemological and empirical point of view, the scientific validity and application of a model of therapeutic intervention. Specifically: - the therapeutic changes obtained are maintained over time, with the possibility of relapses of the disorder reduced to a minimum; as proof of this, the experimental studies conducted with a control group and randomized samples, the video recordings of the therapeutic processes, and the comparison with other therapeutic techniques, i.e. evaluations both qualitative and quantitative (efficacy); - the therapeutic strategy produces results in a reasonably short time, months and not years, otherwise the change could be the effect of fortuitous events (efficiency); - the therapeutic techniques and their process can replicate the results on different subjects who present the same pathology (replicability); - during application, the effects of each single therapeutic maneuver can be predicted within the entire sequence of the model (predictivity); - the model and all its techniques are constantly taught and transmitted to other colleagues so that they can, by applying them, obtain similar results (transmissibility). Initially, the unlocking maneuvers acted by blocking the request for help and protection through a restructuring aimed at creating a greater fear that inhibited the present one, resuming the observation that a greater fear is cornering, and those who hear it often pull out. a winning courage even in the most adverse conditions. To act on avoidant behavior, a series of suggestive prescriptions were devised capable of distracting the subject during exposure to feared situations (counter-avoidances), such as the prescription of the pirouette and that of the apple (Nardone, 1993; 2003). Finally, to stop the attempt to repress one's reactions, the "logbook" was created, that is a sort of apparent monitoring of panic episodes, but actually aimed at producing emotional detachment.

This, starting from the observation that, when the subject reacts to the frightening situation pushed by some reason or stimulus that distracts him from it, he acts without thinking and, only afterwards, he realizes what he has done successfully. Studies on the neurophysiology of panic (Nardone, 2003; 2016) have then highlighted two fundamental processes that occur during a panic attack: on the one hand, the phobic perception involves the limbic system (amygdale, hippocampus, locus coeruleus, hypothalamus ...), which reacts in thousandths of a second, immediately conveying a response to the periphery, activating the "flight or fight " reaction , (or I flee or fight), to which " freezing " has currently been added thanks to the stimulation of the autonomic nervous system, especially the sympathetic section.

On the other hand, after thousandths of seconds, the sensation reaches the cortex, which is responsible for the conscious evaluation of external stimuli and modulates voluntary behaviors; for the amygdale to respond to fear reactions, the medial prefrontal cortex must be deactivated.

The problem arises when the modern mind, hence the cortex, confuses the healthy mechanism described with something dangerous, realizing itself beyond its control, and what scares the most begins to be no longer fear itself, but the reaction of loss. Control of the organism, which leads reason to try to control, and the more it tries to control the more it loses control, up to the physiological tilt of the panic attack. It was therefore necessary to introduce a technique capable of successfully intervening in panic attacks in the absence of a real threatening source, or in those cases in which the frightening threat does not come from outside, but derives from being afraid. Of the fear that triggers the paradoxical escalation to panic. Paradoxically, fear turns into a self-fulfilling prophecy without the need for any external triggering situation.

The technique of the "worst fantasy", the result of constant research-intervention in the field and concrete examples of the success of the paradox fixed in history. We think of the stoic courage of Seneca who, condemned to kill himself by cutting his veins with his own hands and after seeing his wife suffer the same fate before him, managed to overcome fear by spending the period before the execution imagining all the fantasies more terrible about that atrocious horror film of which he would inevitably become the protagonist.

Specifically, the technique consists in asking the person to retire every day to a room where no one can disturb him and, making him comfortable, he will dim the lights and create a soft atmosphere. She will aim for an alarm to go off half an hour later and in this half hour she will begin to immerse herself in all the worst fantasies about what could happen to her. And, in this time, she will do whatever she has to do: if she feels like crying she cries, if she comes from screaming she screams, if she gets to hit the ground she does it. When the alarm goes off... STOP... it's all over; he turns off the alarm, goes to wash his face and goes back to his usual day. So the important thing is that for the whole half hour, whether it does or does not get sick, stay there, lowering him in all the worst that could happen fantasies. He does whatever comes to do, but when the alarm goes off ... STOP... it's all over. He turns off the alarm, washes his face and goes back to his usual day. A half hour of daily passion, then.

The results of the application of the paradoxical injunction to panic (Frankl, 1946) are extraordinary: patients induced to immerse themselves in all the possible worst fantasies about panic, instead of being frightened, relax, creating a counter-paradoxical effect (Nardone, Balbi, 2008) with respect to the paradox of escalation from fear to panic, to the point of sometimes falling asleep. After a rigorous training, which sees the evolution of the technique from half an hour to five minutes five times a day in which the person must make scheduled appointments to their fears to familiarize themselves with the experience for which the more they seek fear, the less it will show up, you come to use the technique before doing something feared (look fear in the face so that it becomes courage") and when fear unexpectedly arises (I touch the ghost when it appears to make it vanish).

In 2000, the evaluation study on 3482 treated cases, of which over 70% suffered from panic attacks, showed a therapeutic efficacy of 95% and with duration of treatments reduced to seven sessions. Hundreds of thousands of cases have been successfully treated since then, with an average success rate in international statistics exceeding 85%. But the most surprising fact is that patients get rid of the invalidating disorder within 3-6 months and that these results, as the follow-up measurements after the end of the therapies show, are maintained over time in the absence of relapses and symptom shifts. This is thanks to the application of an isomorphic logic to that of the persistence of the problem, therefore non-ordinary, and to a form of suggestive persuasive communication. Fear, therefore, if pushed, rather than shunned or repressed, becomes saturated in its own excesses (Nardone, 2016), becoming the clearest demonstration of the fact that "There is no night that does not see day" (Nardone, 2003).

THERAPY FOR ANXIETY DISORDERS

To cure the ' anxiety remedies such as psychological treatment, and in particular the cognitive behavioral therapy, they are very effective results. The therapy cognitive-behavioral is constituted by two components. The first component, cognitive therapy, is one of the most common treatments for treating anxiety. It is based on the idea that our thoughts respond with negative behaviors and feelings to events and situations (often it is not an event that causes discomfort, but the interpretation we make of the particular event).

The purpose of cognitive therapy is to help us identify unnecessary beliefs and thought patterns, which are often automatic, negative and irrational, and replace them with more positive ones and make us, develop critical and rational thinking about the problem.

The second component of cognitive-behavioral therapy involves modifying behaviors that are associated with anxiety and panic attacks, such as avoidance (shirking from something) or restlessness. Learning relaxation techniques are applied to the methods of treating anxiety and induced changes in the way in which certain situations are handled by us.

Therapy may also include other treatments to address and treat anxiety such as anxiolytic medications and lifestyle changes, such as starting exercise, dietary changes with anti-anxiety foods, and reducing caffeine and other exciting foods.

Advice on how to cure anxiety and manage its causes

The causes of extreme anxiety can be due to agitation, stress, panic, fears and tensions. To eliminate this destabilizing problem it is possible to resort to particular methods and natural remedies. To fight anxiety you have to hit the target, understand what really worries you. To find out more, keep reading.

How to fight anxiety: identify stressors for better therapy

The first step in managing and treating anxiety is to identify the specific situations that make us stressed or anxious and when we have coping problems. One way to do this is to keep a diary of symptoms and write what happens to us when you experience the anxiety or panic attack. It is also helpful in identifying any thoughts that worry us more than others and how to go about finding ways to neutralize the specific problem of worry.

We all have a greater ability to handle stressful events than we sometimes imagine, and some self-control techniques improve these skills. Identified situation specification that causes anxiety, the problem-solving is a useful technique to treat anxiety and then the malaise that afflicts us. The problem-solving (problem resolution) involves the following steps:

Identify the problem. After identifying the situations that contribute to our anxiety attacks or panic attacks, we write down the problem and try to be very precise in its description, including what happens to us, where, how, with whom, why, and what we would like. Modify.

We try to come up with as many options as possible to solve the problem. Let's consider the chances of success that these options can help us solve the problem.

We select the option that we consider most appropriate.

We develop a plan to test the chosen option and try to make it happen.

If with the option chosen and implemented we do not get results, remember that we have other options to use.

So let's go back to the list and select the next preferred option.

Breathing exercises to cure anxiety naturally

When those damn anxiety attacks come, we start breathing faster. This rapid breathing leads us to have unpleasant sensations, such as agitation, lightheadedness and mental confusion. Learning a breathing technique to slow breathing can often relieve symptoms and help us think more clearly. It's a very good model to calm down, seeing believes!

The following breathing technique is a natural remedy to stop agitation and fear. Slowing your breathing reduces the symptoms of anxiety. As soon as we feel that our breathing becomes more labored, we apply these 3 rules immediately:

We breathe in through the nose and count 3 seconds and tell ourselves: "IN, two, three".

We always exhale through the nose, and once again we count to three, telling ourselves: "RELAX, two, three".

We keep repeating the exercise for two or three minutes and then breathe normally. Our breathing will have become more regular!

This breathing technique can be used to slow down breathing whenever we feel anxious in any place and without anyone else noticing. They seem like mundane activities but you will discover how they are important pillars to fight anxiety.

Remedies for Anxiety: Relaxation Techniques to Treat Anxiety

When we feel anxious most of the time, calming down and being able to relax seems impossible. Knowing how to release muscle tension is an important treatment for anxiety. Let's relax and have a general feeling of calm, both physical and mental.

Learning a relaxation technique and practicing it regularly can help us maintain a level of anxiety that is easier to manage. You can help make a psychologist or our martial arts teacher to teach us techniques of relaxation, the awareness exercises or other self-taught many ways to learn: how to videos, CDs, books.

Thought Management to calm anxiety

Thought management exercises are helpful when we are troubled by constant or recurring distressing thoughts. There is a wide variety of thought management techniques. For example, gently distracting ourselves by using pleasant thoughts can help us divert our attention from evil thoughts.

Alternatively, we can learn "awareness techniques "to redirect attention from negative thoughts to positive ones. A simple technique is "the substitution of thought" or using the strategies coping. We develop a set of instructions that counter worrying thoughts (for example, "This situation is very difficult but I hold on because it won't last very long"). We replace disturbing thoughts by making reassuring self-statements. The choice of the management technique of thinking depends on the type of anxiety.

Let's change our lifestyle to start treating anxiety

Let's take part in a pleasant daily activity.

It doesn't have to be anything super demanding or expensive, just the little things we like to do and it will be a first step to distract us from worries.

Increase exercise.

Regular exercise helps reduce anxiety by providing a way to eliminate the stress that has built up in our body.

Reduce your caffeine intake.

Caffeine is a stimulant and one of its side effects is to keep us alert and perhaps a little too awake! It also produces the same physiological arousal response that is activated while we are under stress. Less caffeine the fewer reasons available to turn us into anxious.

Reduce your alcohol intake.

Alcohol is often used (unfortunately) to help deal with stress, anxiety and depression. But once the effect of anesthesia passes we will be at the mercy of depression and greater anxiety attacks.

Improve your time management skills.

Let's make sure you have planned some time for rest and for some activities to do in your free time! We must be realistic, the day is not made of 48 hours so, let's lower the pace and resign ourselves to living with calm every now and then!

TIPS FOR ANXIETY RELIEF & MANAGEMENT

One of the secrets to keeping anxiety attacks at bay is being able to control breathing: a very recent study by Stanford University (USA), published in the journal Science, has clarified one of the mechanisms that regulate this state of mind. It is enclosed in a small group of neurons in the brainstem (the part at the base of the brain), which overseas researchers have quickly dubbed "pranayama neurons ".

They are a sort of control unit that detects the rhythm of breathing , in direct communication with the locus coeruleus, the structure of the mind that plays a key role in the state of alertness in general, in focusing attention but, above all, in responses to fear and stress. .

Why panic breaks out and what happens

When your breathing accelerates, which happens when you are tense or fall victim to a panic attack, this "control unit" alerts the locus coeruleus, causing you to enter a state of constant agitation. On the other hand, if you follow a slower pace, you "calm" him and are pervaded by a state of calm.

"In fact, we have long known that there is a close correlation between breathing and emotional disturbances ", explains Professor Giampaolo Perna, psychiatrist and director of the European Center for Anxiety and Emotional Disorders, in Milan and Albese with Cassano (Como).

"The panic attacks, for example, are triggered by a greater sensitivity on the part of sufferers to ' carbon dioxide, one of the gases of respiration. If its levels are even slightly higher than normal they are immediately felt as a choking onset.

Result: you start panting and the increased breathing causes a real escalation of panic symptoms », warns the expert. "Anxiety is a disorder that involves body and mind", relaunches Professor Massimo Biondi, professor of psychiatry at the La Sapienza University of Rome and director of the neuroscience and mental health department of the Policlinico Umberto I in Rome.

What to do? "When we are victims of ' anxiety , in addition to breathe in more accelerated way, we feel the heart racing at a thousand, the front that you sweat pearls, or the muscles of paths tremors . Precisely for this reason, today the most effective therapies are moving on different fronts: not only drugs to re-stabilize the central nervous system, but also relaxation techniques and psychotherapy, which help to become aware and control the physical reactions that put the turbo to restlessness. "

1. Practice breathing with yoga techniques

The first step in the war on anxiety is therefore to learn to control the breath . A goal that can be achieved thanks to meditative practices. Among the yoga techniques there is one, in particular, which has been tested and validated in Italy: it is called Sky, which stands for Sudarshan Kriya Yoga.

It is a variant of the ancient Indian practice, which was the focus of a study conducted by the neuroscience department of the Fatebenefratelli hospital, published in the Journal of Affective Disorders. "It involves the alternation of deep breathing exercises with other faster and more intense ones, which have the effect of inducing a deep state of conscious stillness", explains Professor Claudio Mencacci , president of the Italian Society of Psychiatry and coordinator of the study.

"Within 6 months, this technique has been shown to halve anxiety in 98% of cases. In fact, it manages to rebalance the sympathetic nervous system , responsible for the organic responses (heartbeat, sweating, labored and accelerated breathing), typical of anxious states. In fact, controlling the breath has been shown to help regulate the heartbeat as well, a factor which, in addition to reducing cardiovascular risk, acts as an additional anxiolytic ", explains the expert.

2. Train yourself to "cast out" the thoughts that oppress you

On the control of the breath, but not only, techniques such as transcendental meditation and the most modern mindfulness also aim. Their effectiveness has been demonstrated by new research conducted by the University of Waterloo (Canada) and Harvard University in Cambridge (USA), published in the journal Consciousness and Cognition.

These disciplines, the researchers explain, allow you to focus your attention on the present, thus helping to "drive away" the oppressive and intrusive thoughts typical of anxiety and to regain calm. "A good management of one's mind is also a strong point of bioenergeticsanalysis, ideal psychotherapy because it intervenes both on the body, through physical exercises that help to relieve tension, and on thought", explains Professor Biondi.

"Mental reconditioning can also be used as self-treatment", suggests the expert, who in his manual "Pensieri Terapeutici" illustrates the do-it-yourself techniques to change one's emotional state. For example, saying "you can do it" when you are faced with a difficult situation or thinking, in the event of an accident, "it can happen to anyone", helps to overcome tensions and regain calm.

3. Learn to control heart rhythm

The heart, like breathing, also plays an important role in anxiety disorders. Your body's motor communicates with the brain and its heartbeat significantly affects the way you perceive and react to what happens to you.

"The heart muscle of the anxious is" rigid", therefore not able to adapt and change frequency when emergency situations arise", explains Professor Giampaolo Perna. For this reason, the techniques used to control the heart rhythm and, in general, the vegetative nervous systemis the new strength of cognitive behavioral psychotherapy.

An approach that the international guidelines today indicate as the ideal treatment path against anxiety disorders. To monitor the beats, some therapists use devices that, through sensors applied to the finger or ear, record the pulsations, sending different acoustic signals according to their frequency: the patient becomes aware of them and then, by performing specific exercises, learns to regulate the pulsations, making them more adaptable and functional to psychic well-being.

Or, they use enteroceptic desensitization techniques: those who suffer mainly from panic attacks are very sensitive to the reactions of the body and when they feel them they are immediately frightened.

The therapist, therefore, invites the patient to experience them "safely": he makes him pedal on an exercise bike until his heart is racing, for example, or he invites him to blow into a short straw until he feels that the breath becomes short and labored. Progressively, this exposure to potential physical situations at risk prepares us to recognize and manage the reactions of the body, thus avoiding that they also send the mind "over the top".

4. Trust the right drugs

The techniques that help control physical reactions are accompanied by drugs. The most used are benzodiazepines, useful for "enhancing" the effects of gamma-amino butyric acid (Gaba), a substance produced by the brain that acts as a natural sedative.

There are some fast-acting ones, indicated to overcome the anxiety related to momentary situations that cause fear, such as speaking in public or taking the plane. Others, on the other hand, have a more prolonged and "strong" action, ideal when the malaise lasts for most of the day.

The benzodiazepines , however, are indicated for anxiety states passengers , perhaps linked to an event such as a separation or bereavement, which has removed momentarily calm and relaxation , so do not go well for the forms that do not give up and make it more fragile ", explains Professor Mencacci .

He also remembers to always pay close attention to the use of these medicines: «According to the guidelines of scientific societies, they must be prescribed by the doctor, who also establishes the ideal dosage, and must be taken for no more than 6 weeks.

If the anxiolytic taken for transient anxiety after 2 weeks does not work, it is advisable to switch to another drug, in order to avoid the risk of increasing the doses, perhaps in the name of DIY, in the hope of staying better », warns the expert. Increasing dosages to try to get the desired results can lead to addiction or even addiction.

5. Use antidepressants only if you have a chronic form

If anxiety accompanies you and dominates you every day, you need to focus on tailor-made drugs, such as antidepressants:

«Among those available, paroxetine is one of the most suitable molecules for panic attacks. It allows for a greater availability of serotonin, a neurotransmitter that intervenes on the centers of fear, and influences others such as acetylcholine, important in panic », explains Professor Perna.

"Theduloxetine, however, it is ideal to counteract the generalized anxiety attacks because it allows greater availability of both serotonins, both of norepinephrine, a neurotransmitter that regulates mood, energy and physical responses to anxiety. But pregabaline is equally effective, which acts on the Gaba system, reducing the excitability of neurons and exerting a sedative action », specifies our expert.

However, remember that they must be prescribed by the specialist and do not work right away. It is therefore necessary to wait for the effects with patience, without losing heart:

They are safe medicines and, in general, they are not addictive or addictive. Then, when you feel better (often only 3 months are enough) you can stop, gradually decreasing the dosage.

CONCLUSION

In the meantime, from everything we have seen, it can be said that anxiety is not so much something to "fight" but rather to know and learn to modulate. The first step is to know what it is and how it manifests itself, so that the bodily states experienced do not lead to the triggering of the "fear of fear", exacerbating the anxiety itself.

What Can Help When Suffering From Anxiety?

When anxiety does not have the characteristics of a real disorder, you can start:

Use relaxation techniques, very effective in balancing the activation levels of the body by shifting the psychophysiological balance from a state of activation to a state of relaxation;

Playing sports, because it helps to download the energy levels produced;

Learn to meditate and be aware of the present moment (mindfulnessapproach). Training the mind in awareness helps to control and reduce negative emotions and to know and observe how our mind works;

Curing sleep: anxiety can be amplified by sleep loss, the quality of which has now been shown to be very important for our mental health;

Take care of the quality of personal relationships and social support.

When anxiety reaches more extreme levels of intensity that cannot be controlled by the person, resulting in a real anxiety disorder, professional intervention is required.

How to fight anxiety with professional help

Both anxiolytic and antidepressant drugs are widely used in the treatment of anxiety disorders, but often have problems with addiction and / or side effects as well as not solving the problem at the root.

They have certain effectiveness and can be useful especially in the early stages of therapy, but in many cases their effectiveness is lost upon discontinuation. For this it becomes essential to support them with psychotherapy. A psychotherapeutic path is certainly the best choice and from which it is difficult to ignore.

The cognitive behavioral therapy showed very high efficacy rates and has established itself in the scientific community as the first-line strategy in the treatment of anxiety and its disorders.

To date, when we refer to cognitive behavioral therapy, we mean not only the classical approach, but also its evolutions in recent decades.

Metacognitive Therapy (MCT) to combat anxiety

In cognitive behavioral therapy, much importance has been given to the content of thought, considering it as responsible for the presence of a disorder. The explanation is not entirely exhaustive because negative beliefs do not necessarily lead to emotional suffering that lasts over time.

The therapy metacognitive suggests that dysfunctional emotions derive from metacognition, the process of tracking, monitoring and evaluation of the thought. It seems that metacognitive factors are crucial in determining the harmful and characteristic thinking styles of psychological disorders and the persistence of negative emotions. In fact, a brooding process that is difficult to control is observed in the thought patterns observed in anxiety disorders.

The metacognitive approach therefore directs therapy towards the use of strategies that can enable patients to develop new ways of relating to their thoughts and beliefs. Stop brooding that support is essential to effectively fight anxiety.

ACCEPTANCE & COMMITMENT THERAPY (ACT) TO DEAL WITH ANXIETY

People suffering from anxiety, panic, fears, catastrophic thoughts, brooding feel frustrated, damaged, limited, and with catastrophic expectations of their future. It is clear that all this leads people to try in every way to "free themselves" from anxiety ".

The Acceptance and Commitment Therapy (ACT) approach, on the other hand, starts from the assumption that anxiety is "part" of life and must not become "the whole life".

This means learning not to continually struggle with anxiety, continuing to feed it further. This is to make sure that anxiety is not constantly in the foreground and does not prevent you from continuing to walk your path towards what you really want.

This approach basically teaches you to let go of what you cannot control and take back control instead of what you can control. Often we cannot control the thoughts that come to our mind, but instead have a choice about how we relate to them. We can choose to let them pass and experience them simply for what they are: thoughts, feelings, memories...

It's not about fighting anxiety better or harder, but about changing how you relate to it. You can learn to accept anxiety and the thoughts that accompany it with kindness and compassion, thus reducing its negative charge. Choosing to stop fighting with negative emotion and engage in concrete and constructive action.

Finally seven moves to free you from anxiety

Robert Leahy in his book of 2007 concretizes and summarizes many of these concepts in "Seven moves to free you from anxiety". After understanding how it works and what leads to intensifying restlessness and anxiety it is good:

- determine when to worry and when not
- accept the reality and commit to change
- putting into question their thinking style dominated restlessness
- focus on what is the deepest threat
- transform "failure" into opportunity
- use emotions instead of worrying about them
- take control of the weather